Put Comfortable Shoes in My Coffin

True Stories of Faith, Family, and Fortitude

By Jennifer Girardi McCloskey

with Mary Rey Girardi

Put Comfortable Shoes in My Coffin: True Stories of Faith, Family, and Fortitude

By Jennifer Girardi McCloskey

© 2019 Jennifer Girardi McCloskey

Printed in the United States of America

ISBN: 978-1-7339405-0-4

Published by: The Ghost Publishing

Edited by: Lil Barcaski

Proofread by: Linda Hinkle

Contact info: Jennifer McCloskey, Jennifer.mac1@gmail.com

Cover Design: Erin Girardi

Dedication

This book is dedicated to my father, who taught me I could do anything, and to my mother, who cheered in my every attempt.

Table of Contents

Introduction

One Thanksgiving, I had somehow managed to arrange three long tables to accommodate seating for our twenty-seven family members so we could all eat together. We spilled into the living room and hallway to take our seats, sharing laughter and stories as the turkey was passed up and down the long stretch of tables. I heard my cousin, John, speaking to my niece, Erin, about my father who had served in the Military. Erin, who listened intently, sang out, "Wow, Pop-Pop was amazing!" I shared in her excitement and told another story about my dad's Military experience.

I described an event when my father had saved a man's life, and as I told my recollection of the story with as much specific detail as I could remember, my cousin, John, noted he had never heard about my dad's heroism. He whole-heartedly said, "You should write these stories down!" Erin agreed, and the seed was planted.

So, here I sit at my computer, in my 98-year-old Mom's kitchen, listening to her stories as she bakes the world's best chocolate chip cookies. My goal is to remind all of us there are heroes all around us; all we have to do is notice. These stories are my recollection of events I've personally experienced, and those told to me by family members and friends. I have learned there is strength in the big things in life, as well as the little things, and success can be saving a life or planting a garden. I believe the greatest gifts we can receive are faith, family, and fortitude, and they are all defined by love.

So, as I write down these events, these stories, which not only surround me, but make me who I am today, I am forever grateful for their existence and for their continuous lessons.

Thank you, Mom and Dad, for giving me a faith, my family, and the fortitude and strength of character to know when I am blessed.

Chapter 1

The Sweater

"Memories of our lives, of our works and our deeds will continue in others." Rosa Parks

"What is this thing?" I asked my mom, as I pulled a piece of cloth from a dust covered bag. She and I and my sister Janell were cleaning out the basement of my family home and gathering items to donate to charity. I'd been working my way from box to bag, finding memory after memory. Mom didn't look up at first, head down rummaging through some papers.

"It looks so old. I doubt they'll take this. Should we toss it?" I asked, talking to her back. "It looks like some kind of old funny-colored sweater," I said, gingerly pulling a wrinkled dingy brownish garment from the bag. My nose crinkled from the musty smell, as I held it up with two fingers and crossed the room to my mom. When my mother turned to see what I was holding, the look on her face told me this was more than just an old piece of clothing. She gently pulled it away from me and pressed it

13

to her cheek. Her eyes closed, as she leaned into the sweater as if she were resting her head against the chest of a lover.

"This was your Father's World War II Army sweater. The military called this color *olive drab*. Isn't it beautiful?" she said softly. "This sweater holds many stories," she continued. "Your father wore this during his time fighting in Germany," she added.

A soldier. I'd never thought of my father as a soldier. He was just my father. He had always been *My dad*, the man who loved us unconditionally, the man who went to work every day, as vice president of his company, the man who was simply, my friend. Honestly, I had never really thought of him prior to being *my dad*. Looking at my mother's face and her winsome smile, suddenly I envisioned her as a young woman, who affectionately loved a handsome soldier, hoping he would return to her. The sweater was more than a dingy, old, colored piece of cloth. It was a part of their history, and so, in a sense, a part of mine. Mom had memories I would never be part of or know. For the first time I realized, before these people were our father and mother they were once simply, Jim and Mary, two young people with lives full of hopes and dreams, and I wanted, very much, to know more about them.

Chapter 2

Someone Likes Them

"Survival can be summed up in three words—never give up. That's the heart of it really. Just keep trying."
Bear Grylls

My Mother, Mary Civita Rey, was born in 1921. Her parents, Michael Pasquale Rey and Mary LaMonica Rey, had immigrated from Italy years earlier with the hopes of raising a family in America, the land of opportunity. My mother, their fourth born child, was very special. She was not only named after her mother, she was a student of life, watching and learning from everyone she met and always seeking to be of use. She studied her father's every move, as he crushed the grapes from their own vines to make the family wine in the basement of their Pennsylvania home. She learned to be resourceful by helping in the kitchen, as her Mother used every single last piece and part of the chicken in the meals she prepared for the week. "God made every part of the animal for something, Mary. Find a use for all of it," her mother would remind her.

Italians have a great love for the bounty of the earth. Italy is replete with vegetables, lemons, and fruit – especially grapes and tomatoes. Growing up in an Italian household, Mom always tended a garden in her backyard. She learned the value of growing your own food and, to this day, she keeps a garden in her yard. Her garden produces everything from tomatoes, peppers, and zucchini, to select fruits. She takes tender care of her garden, nurturing and watering it daily. As her bounty blossoms and is ready to harvest, my mother shares its many gifts. One day, we were picking the ripe peppers from their stems and I remembered my mother didn't eat peppers. She didn't like them. "Mom, you don't like peppers. Why do you grow them?" I asked.

"Someone likes them," she said, with a tender smile.

Mom and her siblings had many chores. There was always something to keep them busy and helpful around the house. As a young girl, Mom learned to wrap the young tomato plants from their family garden in newspaper, since they had no pots, and take them to the local market to sell. When she returned home, she would hand the money she made from their sale to her mother, but she would often keep a nickel after each trip. This was not for herself, or to be selfish, but she would save each nickel, so she could surprise her mother later, when money was scarce. How proud she would be when she was able to hand over a dollar for her mom to buy a little extra meat or milk when times were rough.

My mother's mom came to America from Italy, where she had learned to use tomatoes in many ways. Making fresh sauce was a family tradition, and ripe, fresh tomatoes from your own garden meant the old sauce in the new world.

My mom was in her early teens when the Depression occurred, and even in her small town of Scottsdale, Pennsylvania, the effects were felt deeply. Feeding the family was extremely important and the garden and its harvest were critical. Mom remembers canning every kind of vegetable and fruit, and sometimes, even meat. Waste not, want not. Her father worked in the local coal mines, but the work depended on the seasons and was not steady. Her family would save and store food as much as possible to prepare for economic uncertainty, in times when work was scarce. Nothing was wasted, everything was used.

My mom remembers what it means to experience real hunger pains. Because of this, she never allowed any of her children use the term, "starving." "Mom! When are we going to eat? I'm starving," one of us would say.

"You don't know the meaning of the word *starving*, don't ever use that word lightly," she would remind us.

Henry David Thoreau said, "A man is rich in proportion to the number of things he can live without." My mother understood this concept inherently. When I was young, my Mother would tell us these stories and we realized her family had very little money, but they found a way.

Our Italian family always loved to visit and spend time together. I remember Mom telling me, when company would arrive, and she, being the youngest, would give up her bed for the guests. She would sleep in the kitchen on an old chair, her pillow just a coat rolled up in an old pillowcase. This story stayed with me, not because of the sacrifice my mother made, but because of her unbridled willingness to do so. In telling me this story, I never felt she was saddened by the event, but she accepted it as part of her responsibility, and something she could offer as a gift to visiting guests and family.

The stories of Mom's childhood remind me to give as freely as my mother did, and to give of yourself without a request for sympathy or expectation of reward.

A student was talking to his teacher, and the student said, "Now I understand, the strong man dies but once, the weak man dies a thousand times."

"No," the teacher replied, "The strong man dies a thousand times too, you just never know it."

Chapter 3

One Roller Skate

"Let us sacrifice our today so that our children can have a better tomorrow." A.P.J. Abdul Kalam

Growing up, my mom loved to roller skate, a fact that did not escape my grandmother. Mom found an old skate someone had thrown away, and she and her brother, John, manipulated it so they could clamp it on to one of their shoes. They took turns rolling lopsidedly up and down the streets, on the one skate, throughout their neighborhood. Mom learned to manipulate that single skate almost like a skateboard, gliding on it on one foot and pushing off the pavement with the other. It was a complicated and delicate task, maintaining balance while gaining speed and momentum. Every day, my Grandmother would watch my Mom as she one-foot skated, practically everywhere she went, her skill level rising rapidly.

Mary would help her Mother carry groceries from the local market, one-foot skating as she returned. Mom said her mother was always concerned watching, with bated breath, as her daughter tried to balance groceries and maneuver between people and cars on the walk/skate home. "Be careful, Mary. Watch for cars and be careful not to crush the eggs or bread," my grandmother would warn.

My grandmother participated in a Grocery Club, a type of market where you could earn points toward various different prizes. She was saving these points to purchase new kitchen utensils to assist her in the chore of cooking, three times a day, for a family of six. They were a very low-income family and mom remembers having to come home from school for lunch every day, to a fried egg and toast. She knew her mother needed to budget the family money and often watched as my grandmother counted pennies to ensure they had enough food for the week, enough to feed six hungry mouths, this was no easy task.

One afternoon, Mom came home from school to find her mother had already left for the market. She went outside to wait for her to return so she could assist with the bags. She saw her mother walking toward the house with the groceries. Mom went to greet her on her one-foot skate, propelling herself effortlessly forward, down the middle of the street. When she reached her, my grandmother handed her a bag with something heavy inside, almost like metal. Mary knew this was odd, since her mom had just been to the grocery store.

What could she have purchased that was made of metal at a grocery store? Mary pondered. Mary looked inside the bag, and there, shiny and bright, were *two* brand-new roller-skates.

Stunned at this discovery, Mary shouted, "Mom, what are these for?"

"They're for you," her mother replied.

"But how?" Mary squealed.

"The Grocery Club offered them as a prize!" her Mother explained. She knew how much Mary loved to skate and was worried about the thought that she would get hurt maneuvering on her one skate.

"But Mama, you needed those points for the kitchen things!" Mary insisted.

"Your joy means more than all of those kitchen tools combined," her mother whispered. "My joy will be watching your face when you skate with those on your two feet. Just think how much easier it will be to carry the groceries now."

My mother never forgot those skates, or what my grandmother had sacrificed to provide them for her. She could have used those points for things to make her life easier, but she chose to make my mother's life brighter.

That is a kind of love no amount of money can buy.

Chapter 4

Perception

"I can't change the direction of the wind, but I can adjust my sails to always reach my destination." Jimmy Dean

Growing up, my mom had many jobs. She was employed by a local convenience store which, in those days, was usually called a Five and Dime Store. When she received her paycheck, she would buy three pounds of ground beef for her mother to make meals for the family, giving the remainder of her paycheck to her mom, with the exception of one dollar. She would save her dollars for months until she was able to afford to buy herself a new dress.

World War II changed the daily life of so many people in the states. Civil defense and production of goods needed for the war effort became the focus for many factories, especially in the East. The economy shifted from domestic industry, to defense. As young men left for war, women were needed to fill the gap in the labor force, and they did so with gusto and pride. Mom heard there were jobs in Baltimore, Maryland, paying much more than the Five and

Dime, so she and her sister Rose headed to Baltimore and went to work for the Glen L. Martin Company, at their plant designing airplanes for World War II.

Mom and Rose told us how they were expected to dress professionally for work every day. Due to limited resources in those days, nylon stockings were scarce. Before the war, women always wore nylon hose with a seam along the back. This was still the fashion in 1942, but now the nylon was being used in the war effort, and stockings were no longer available. Women not wearing hose at work were considered unprofessional, which posed a dilemma for Mom and Aunt Rose. Once their well-worn stockings had worn out, finding replacements were difficult and costly. So, Mom and Aunt Rose used their ingenuity. They used a yardstick and eyebrow pencil to draw the, "seam" along the back of each other's legs to give the illusion of wearing the required hose. No one ever noticed they were actually bare-legged. Years later, I so appreciated their resourcefulness. It has taught me to always, "find-a-way."

Chapter 5

The Chalked Floor

"When we seek to discover the best in others, we somehow bring out the best in ourselves." William Arthur Ward

The Glen L. Martin Company designed and built airplanes during World War II. The company employed aeronautical engineers as their designers, as well as mechanical engineers and machinists who built the actual airplanes. My father, a young, vibrant self-starter, James Anthony Girardi, ran the machine shop's night crew. With him leading the way, his team continuously produced excellent results. One morning, the machine shop's day crew supervisor, was studying the night crew's production sheets and was impressed with their outstanding production, but had a concern about his own crew's work. At the end of his shift, as the night crew entered the shop, the day crew supervisor approached my dad and whispered, "Jim, would you mind slowing your men down a little, you're making my men on the day crew look bad."

Jim was surprised by the request. Taken aback, he searched the day crew supervisors face to determine if he was joking, but quickly realized he was quite sincere and honestly worried about how his men would be judged. Though dad understood the concern, he replied, "I'm afraid I can't do that. This company is paying me to do the best job I can. There is a certain amount of pride you take in everything you do. I can't slow my men down to make others look good," he replied.

Later that night, Jim shared the earlier discussion he had with his night crew team and they developed an idea. The next morning, when the day crew entered the machine shop, they were welcomed with something different. On this morning, they were greeted by a large number *seven* scribed in chalk on the concrete floor. It didn't take long for the day crew to realize what this cryptic message meant. The night crew was telling them they had completed seven units the night before. Jim's amazing team was producing and challenging their fellow workers.

Later that same evening, when Jim's crew returned to work, they found the chalked number, seven had been erased and the number eight was scribed in its place. From that day forward, the competition was in full swing and Jim's crew not only continued outstanding production, but the day crew did as well. The results were amazing. A simple number on the floor represented a mentality of strength, determination, and pride.

My father's mentality reminds me to always challenge myself and to raise the number, day by day.

Chapter 6

The Comfort of a Candle

"There are two ways of spreading light: to be the candle or the mirror that reflects it." Edith Wharton

My cousin Marianne was born in the 1940s. She was born premature, to my mom's sister, Gaetana, and doctors did not have the prenatal tools and medicines of today to care for her small body. My mother remembers the doctors sending Marianne home to die. She was too little to survive, and there was nothing more they could do for her. My grandmother said this child would not die, and went into action.

Marianne's parents brought her home to find that my grandmother had turned on the oven in anticipation. Once warmed, the oven was warm enough for her mission, she turned the oven off, and placed a special blanket inside. Once the blanket was warm, they wrapped Marianne in it and held her very close. The family took turns heating the blanket and wrapping Marianne's little body in the warmth. They would often sit in front of the open oven, as it gave off heat, and rock the tiny baby girl to sleep. They fed her milk with an eyedropper as often as her little body requested.

Marianne did not die that cold December week in the 1940s, she did not die the following week; she survived. No one believed she had made it through the winter. Slowly, she continued to grow in strength and in wisdom.

Marianne grew into a very bright and inquisitive young girl. Unfortunately, my Aunt Gaetana died very young, when Marianne was only ten years old. Growing up with a demanding father and missing her mother, life was difficult. Marianne remembers an evening when she was saddened by the events at her home, her frustration had grown, and she needed to find peace. Without a thought, she left her house and walked into the night, wanting to be anywhere but there. Having nowhere specific to go, she wandered into a nearby church.

She knelt in a pew and had a long talk with God. Although feeling somewhat better about her situation, and feeling comforted, she was still not ready to return home. She remembers the church becoming cold as night fell. The church grew dark, with the exception of a single candle, someone had lit earlier in the evening. Her eyes were drawn to it. She lifted herself off the pew she had been sitting in and wandered over to the candle. The candle sat among the section of the church, where several candles where placed for members of the congregation to light during a special prayer request. She felt the warmth of the one candle, and so she lit another and another. She lit all the candles in that area, in an attempt to stay warm. Sitting near the warmth of the candles that surrounded her, she drifted off to sleep. She remembers feeling calm and warm and no longer alone. She woke early the next morning with a new view on life. She now carried herself with the strength of a new day and the knowledge that she was comforted both spiritually, and physically that night.

There was a greater plan for Marianne since the moment she was born. Marianne is now a prominent pediatrician, with a sub specialty of adolescent medicine, and has been a well-respected Physician-in-chief at various universities and hospitals where she teaches, authors, and works. Whether her comfort came from the warmth of an oven or the light from a candle, she spreads her warmth, love, and kindness to this day. The gift of life she was given, she returns many times over.

Chapter 7

Rooftop Romance

"The most important thing a father can do for his children, is to love their mother." Theodore Hesburgh

Even amidst a war, Mom and Dad (young Mary and Jim) knew life shouldn't be just about work. There was a time and place for work, and a time and place for play. They worked diligently, but they also made time for fun when the work week ended.

Dad's night crew completed their shift around 11 p.m. every night and on weeknights most of the men returned home and rested for the next nights shift. However, on Thursday nights, they exhaled, ready to dance at the almost-end of a long, tough week. The young men would quickly shower, change into their party clothes, and gather on the rooftop of the local YMCA. The day crew, where Mom worked, as an aeronautical engineer, after receiving a certificate from the state university, would join them. Mom, and many other women, were trained in the technical trades to assist the Martin Company, while so many young men were called into the service.

The young women's shift ended around 5 p.m., so they would head home for a nap after work, then dress up and join the machinists at midnight on the YMCA roof. Music would be playing under the stars and there was always plenty of food and dancing. They would laugh, and dance, and share stories. More often than not, the party would last all night, and the men would walk the women home early the next morning, just in time for them to dress and head to work. Jim always volunteered to walk Mary home. "I think Jim likes you, Mary," her sister whispered. Mary just smiled. *Maybe*, she thought, but wasn't sure. He was always a gentleman and quite handsome, but she wasn't yet certain of his feelings for her.

One early morning, on the quiet walk home, my Mom decided to light herself a cigarette, but she fumbled with the match, and in an instant, the whole pack of matches caught fire and burned her hand. "Ouch!" she said sharply, dropping the blazing pack to the ground, and stomping out the fire with her foot.

"Did you burn yourself?" Jim asked. "Let me see."

Mary, being very stoic, insisted she was fine.

"It's nothing, Jim," she replied and didn't allow him to see where she had burned her hand.

In a few minutes, they reached her building. Jim walked her right to the door of the basement apartment she shared with her sister and they said their goodnights. About a half an hour later, there was a soft knock at Mary's window. It was Jim. He had found an all-night pharmacy and had purchased salve and gauze to dress Mary's burn.

"Jim! You scared me," Mom said as she slid open the window. "What are you doing back here?"

"I came to the window so I wouldn't wake Rose," Jim whispered softly. "Here, I thought you might need these." He handed her the package through the window and disappeared into the night before she could properly thank him. Mary was grateful for the salve and gauze, but even more grateful for his generosity. He made an impression with that simple gesture. My future father had just exhibited something very important. He showed Mary he knew what it meant to be kind and loving. Love is about actions, not about words. Love is putting someone else's needs before your own, and that night Jim did. He could have just gone home and rested rather than traipse the neighborhood looking for something to comfort Mary. He made the right choice and showed her his true self.

Mom knew any man who puts others needs first, is a man she would want to get to know better, and she did. After that night, Mary and Jim became inseparable. A few months later, Jim received a draft letter to report for service for World War II. Without hesitation, Jim proposed to Mary and she full-heartedly accepted.

Chapter 8

The Cathedral

"Keep your face always toward the sunshine—and shadows will fall behind you." Walt Whitman

My mother and father were married in Baltimore, Maryland in late August of 1944. Two weeks after they said their vows, my father went to boot camp in Florida, in preparation of deployment to Germany during World War II. My mother wrote to him every day, during his time at boot camp. They had arranged for her to visit him once boot camp was completed, prior to his deployment, for Christmas. In preparation of her arrival, my father worked extra shifts, so he could have significant time off to spend with his bride. He even worked night shifts, so he could spend the three days she was in town solely with her.

The Saturday evening she was to arrive, my father reserved a beautiful hotel room, bought flowers for the nightstand, and tried to make everything perfect for her arrival. At the appointed time of the evening she was to arrive, excited and anxious, he ran to the train station only to learn her train had been delayed from 7:00 p.m. that evening, until midnight. He didn't allow himself to be disappointed, instead, he returned to the hotel room and tried to read to distract himself from waiting. Anxiously he returned at midnight, only to learn that once again, her train was delayed and would not arrive until 3:00 a.m. Sunday morning. Exhausted, he returned at 3:00 a.m., and was told this time the train would now arrive an additional four hours later at 7:00 a.m. Frustrated and sleep deprived, Jim went back to the hotel to wait again. He was extremely worried he would fall asleep and not wake up in time to meet Mary at the station, so he sat in a chair next to the bed, allowing only his head to rest on the edge of the bed in an effort to sleep lightly. He lay in this odd and uncomfortable position, trying to stay semi-awake, but the long work hours, demanding job, and his weary body gave way to an immediate and deep slumber.

He awoke, Sunday morning, as the rays of sun entered his window. In a state of immediate panic, he opened his eyes and shot up from the chair. Blurry eyed, he reached for his glasses and focused on the clock. "Eight o'clock, I've missed her!" He hurried out the door, and ran to the train station, looking wildly for Mary, but she was nowhere in sight. He rushed to the man at the train depot desk, "Was a beautiful blonde here waiting for someone?" he gasped.

"Why, yes," replied the attendant. "She was pacing in a pair of stiletto heels. She waited for a long while, then picked up her bags, thanked me, very politely, and left."

"Did she say where she was going?"

"No. Sorry pal."

My father ran from the station looking in every window of every coffee house and diner, up and down every street, peering down every walkway, in the hope he would find his bride. He searched for my mom for what seemed like an eternity. *I've let her down,* he thought to himself. *She knows no one, she was counting on me to meet her and take her to a hotel, and now she is lost in a city she knows nothing about. I have failed her. Now what?* Cell phones had not yet been invented, and they had only communicated via letters previously, so he was left feeling helpless and worried. After hours of searching, alone and defeated, he wandered into a local cathedral and knelt in the back corner of a church pew to pray. He dropped his head into his hands and asked God to help him, as the tears fell silently from his face.

Soon, the church began to fill with attendees. Families and soldiers took their places in the pews, ready for Sunday morning services. My father, who had settled into his own conversation with God, was awoken from his reverie by the familiar sound of stiletto heels walking down the marble aisle of the church. He lifted his head, and turned to see my mother walking down the center aisle to take a seat in a front pew. My father, relieved and thrilled to see her, immediately rose and did what any man who hadn't seen his bride in four months would have done. He ran back to the hotel, shaved, brushed his teeth and hair, scurried back to the church, and slid in next to her, in her pew, where they had a wonderful and heartfelt reunion.

The real lesson of this story came years later. When I heard about the delayed train story as a child, I asked my mom what she was thinking when Dad didn't meet her at the station. Mom could have acted as a victim and said she was worried and scared, or she could have blamed my dad and said he should have been there for her. None of those were her response. Instead she said, almost in passing, "I knew he'd find me, I wasn't worried."

"How could you not be worried, what did you do?" I asked her.

"I went and found a hotel room, combed my hair, and went to church," she responded. In Mom's mind, you just take care of things, no drama, and have plenty of hope. Prepare for what you need, and live your life. I have always tried to emulate my mother and the strength she showed on that day. Even now, almost thirty years after my father's passing, my mother does exactly what she did that Sunday morning in the train station. She takes care of her home, she takes care of her hair, she goes to the hairdresser every Friday like clockwork, and she goes to church. She has always had the attitude of, *I can do this, no problem.*

When I asked my mom why she married Dad right before he went to war, she thoughtfully replied, "I wanted to give him something to live for." My siblings and I are so glad she did.

Chapter 9

The Canteen

"A river cuts through rock, not because of its power, but because of its persistence." James N. Watkins

My mother asked my father to share with his children an event from his time served in World War II. She felt this would help us greater understand my father's character. My father explained how his unit was on a mission, which included crossing a small, rickety bridge, in their Jeeps. As the group of men in their Jeeps crowded the bridge, it suddenly began to sway, the wood beneath their tires made loud cracking sounds.

"The bridge is collapsing!" The men were yelling and shouting to one another as the make-shift bridge collapsed under their weight, plunging them and the vehicles into the icy water beneath.

The soldiers jumped from their Jeeps as water poured in and began pulling and pushing one another from the freezing river, until everyone made it safely to shore. "Take a head count fellas," their sergeant bellowed. "Are we all here? Everyone make it?"

The men took stock, counting and checking their ranks to ensure they were all present, but they quickly realized one man was missing.

"Sarge! John's not on the shore," someone shouted.

Many of the men immediately jumped into the frigid water looking for their companion. Time ticked away, and they began to fear the worst; the missing man was gone. Refusing to give up on John, my father continued to dive under, deeper and deeper, while many other exhausted soldiers flung themselves on the river bank, too tired to continue. Jim went under again, and through the murky water, felt a strap; yes, a canteen strap. The drowning soldier had his canteen slung across his body. Jim recognized the feel of the strap and yanked on it as hard as he could loosening his comrade from the grip of the deep water. Jim pulled John all the way to shore by that thin canteen strap. One of the men performed mouth-to-mouth resuscitation on the man and saved his life. Thanks to my father, John survived to fight another day.

That story demonstrated to me and my siblings the strength of perseverance and the selflessness those men had, in not giving up on a lost friend. I think of this story whenever I get tired or want to give up. My father was always my hero, but this story reminds me of one of the many reasons why.

Chapter 10

Sparkplug Sensibility

"It's not that I'm so smart, it's just that I stay with problems longer." *Albert Einstein*

Not all of my father's experiences in war were traumatic. There were calmer moments during his World War II days, when soldiers had a chance to rest and find the calmness of the day. He told us of nights he would spend laughing and relaxing with the men at the local pub.

The pub was very popular, and many soldiers would become quite inebriated and try to drive back to the base. Not always in the best condition when leaving, soldiers would hop in any Jeep available, since no keys were needed, and head back to the base. Often the return trip was not in the same Jeep they had arrived in.

My father witnessed this happening too many times. Knowing each man was accountable for the Jeep they had signed out, and being a brilliant mechanic, Dad had a simple and effective solution. He would pull the spark plug from his vehicle when he parked. It was small enough to fit in his pocket, and there was no chance of any of his inebriated pals driving his Jeep back to the base by mistake. When he returned to his Jeep at the end of the evening, he would pop the sparkplug back in place and return to base.

Sometimes the easiest way is the best way.

Chapter 11

The Backdoor

"What lies behind you and what lies in front of you, pales in comparison to what lies inside of you." Ralph Waldo Emerson

Dad was often reluctant to share his stories, of his time as a soldier in World War II, because it was a difficult time. As a young child, I tried to comprehend the intensity of his tour, and though it was difficult at times, one story reminded me of the seriousness of war.

My dad's unit was working their way through a small deserted town. Dad and another soldier were ordered to enter a building to make sure it was secure. He and his buddy covered one another, and they ran to the front door of the building to ensure no one was inside. The building was dark and quiet, but something didn't seem right. An odd feeling of unease came over my dad, and he immediately paused.

He motioned to Herb, his buddy, making quiet gestures to inform him they should enter through the back, so they did. Slowly, they pushed on the heavy wood of the back door, and surprisingly, it swung open freely. They stormed through the opening and into the building, guns ready, searching every room for any sign of movement, all senses on high alert. They searched every crevice of the building, for what seemed like an eternity. After several intense minutes, they determined the building was clear of enemy personnel, and secure for their unit to enter. Finally, Herb and Dad approached the front door and were startled.

They discovered it had wires and an odd mechanism attached. It had been booby-trapped. If one of them had entered through the front door, they would have been killed. My father and his buddy stared wide-eyed at each other and exhaled long deep breaths. Thank God my father had trusted his instincts. He was grateful for the uneasy feeling that saved his life and Herb's.

My father told this story very light heartedly; however, I know if he had gone through that door, I would not have been sitting before him listening to his words, nor would my three siblings.

I remind myself of this story when faced with a difficult challenge. It reminds me to go around through the backdoor, when times get tough, or when a more cautious approach might be needed. It reminds me to follow my gut if something feels wrong or uneasy. Sometimes, we may want to consider talking to someone gently, or allow for other options in lieu of barreling into a situation with full force.

It reminds me to trust my gut feelings. They just might be lifesaving.

Chapter 12

Find-a-Way

"Try to be a rainbow in someone's cloud." Maya Angelou

My father worked at a military airport during his time in the National Guard. One night, the electricity went out at the airport and several planes were diverted to alternate airports because, without electricity, there was no proper lighting for the runway. An airman scheduled to land at my father's airstrip radioed Dad's control tower, noting he was low on fuel and would not be able to divert. "Sorry gentlemen, I have no other option," the pilot reluctantly voiced over the radio. "I have to land with you, even if it's in the pitch dark."

The pilot would attempt to land at Dad's airfield and would need to do his best to land the plane safely. Upon hearing this, with little time to spare, Dad and his team went to work. They aligned Jeeps on either side of the runway, with their headlights turned on, angling the vehicles so the lights would not blind the pilot as he descended. They quickly hung a white bed sheet from the local barracks at the end of the runway, and shined several

Jeep lights onto the sheet so the pilot would know where the end of the runway was located.

The pilot aligned his descent and lowered his landing gear, while the entire airport crew watched in anticipation. He performed a perfect landing that night, perfectly positioned between the Jeeps, manned by the crewman who were hollering with joy. The young pilot jumped from his plane and shook the hand of every man on that airstrip who helped illuminate his arrival. He told my dad, "When I turned the corner and saw the airfield beautifully lit, I was amazed. I thought you had lost power. This airfield was better lit than most of the fully functional ones where I land!"

When it seemed impossible, they found a way. I remind myself every day, "Find a way, be someone's light."

Chapter 13

War

"The supreme art of war is to subdue the enemy without fighting." Sun Tzu

My father would often drive his nephews home from church. One afternoon, he was driving my cousin, John, through Baltimore on the return trip home. John was in third grade and remembers talking to my dad about his time spent in the Army. As a very young man, John was enthralled, as Dad answered John's questions about his time in Germany. John was very inquisitive and absorbed any details Dad provided. They passed a memorial and John expressed his respect and admiration for those who had served, but with the acknowledgment of a third grader he said, "That war was stupid."

Dad became quiet and said softly to his nephew, "All war is stupid."

They sat quietly for a few minutes as they drove. The air was thick, but neither wanted to break the solemn moment. John knew my father's intent even as a third grader. He knew the pride my dad carried with him and the loyalty he had to his country, but he also pondered what my father must have seen and experienced to have made the remark. John has never forgotten those words, and as he now watches, his son, David, serve our country, he knows the intensity of their true meaning.

Chapter 14

Think Big

"Shoot for the moon and if you miss you will still be among the stars." Les Brown

My father was an amazing salesman. For several years in a row, during the early days of his career, he was awarded *Top Sales Producer* for his company. When I was old enough to fully understand the impact of his achievement, I asked him the secret of his success. "Jen, it's all about attitude. If you want to sell two rolls of carpet, go in to work in the morning with the mindset you could sell three rolls, then double that expectation in your mind!" he said.

This mantra would be recited in his head, right before he would walk into a store, "Think big, and double it." He told me how his clients would come in thinking they were going to buy two rolls of carpet, but Dad would somehow sell them six. The key to selling is to truly believe in the product or service you are selling. It was to remember, what you are selling is more than carpet, it's someone's comfort, elegance, and joy. He loved his company's products, and it showed. He exuded confidence when on the sales floor, and it was contagious. The customers wanted what he was selling, and because he believed in it so much, they couldn't help but agree with him.

Integrity, honesty, and confidence will always win big.

Chapter 15

Actions not Words

"Love begins at home, and it is not how much we do...but how much love we put in that action." Mother Teresa

As a Catholic teenager, Mom celebrated Confirmation. This is a sacrament where we renew our baptismal vows and, select a model or Saint we wish to emulate throughout our lives. Mom selected St. Louise. St. Louise was dedicated to caring for the sick, the poor, and the neglected. So is my mother. I've watched her do so, selflessly, my entire life. Mom selected the perfect Saint to emulate as her model. My mother has visited more sick people, and has also been to more funerals, than anyone I know.

"Care for the living, but respect the dead," she would say.

When someone would pass away, she would always remind me to do something kind for the family. "Don't say, let me know if you need anything," Mom would tell me. "No one will ever tell you they are lonely, or hungry, or in need of a kind word. Just do it." She reminded me to bring them something, and leave it at their door, call them on holidays, or send a card telling them you are thinking of them. Just show up and sit with them. Actions are always far better than words and will help people heal and feel comforted.

One afternoon, Mom received a phone call. Her friend Betty from the neighborhood had died. My mom immediately went to their home, she hugged Betty's daughter and sat with her for a few minutes while the grieving daughter shared memories of her mom's last few days. Other neighbors began to arrive sharing their condolences. Mom quietly excused herself, came home and began to cook. She prepared a meal for Betty's family, she prepared cookies and breads for Betty's daughter, to provide for all those who would be stopping by in the next few days.

And she made soup. Lots of soup. Soup for the family to eat, over the long difficult week. Soul-warming soup for them to share, as they remembered their mother. Soup to offer visitors, who came to pay their respects. Sometimes food can mean more than just something to eat. Sometimes just showing up can mean more than words.

Doing something means love.

Chapter 16

Her Belief

"Be strong, be fearless, be beautiful. And believe that anything is possible, when you have the right people there to support you." Misty Copeland

My sister, Janell, and I shared a room when I was young. She knew me well; sometimes better than I knew myself. At times, she was both a sister and a mother to me, because of the seven-year difference in our ages. Her wisdom was immense, but I didn't appreciate her insight until I was in middle school.

I remember my excitement preparing for the Friday night dance. Discussions at the bus stop and the classroom all centered around the upcoming dance. My friends and I laughed in anticipation of all the events the night would unfold. We were excited about the guys in our class, who were planning to attend, we were predicting who would be dating by the end of the evening. The anticipation grew, and Friday night finally arrived. The dance started out slow. Young middle-school gentlemen on one side of the gym, and young ladies on the other. As the music continued, nervous young men asked the ladies to dance, and as the lights dimmed, everyone was connecting with a partner. I watched. There were no cell phones to become lost in, there were no Ubers to take me home. Just me, watching as every one of my friends was asked to dance at one point in the night. I acted excited for them, as they would return to the bleachers, and describe how they were asked to dance, and how the music played during their dance was their new favorite song. I listened and pretended to share in their delight.

I returned home that night, humbled and quiet. My sister, who had witnessed my pre-dance excitement, asked me if I had been asked to dance. "No," I replied softly, with my head held low.

Quick to respond, Janell said, "You know Jen, sometimes the prettiest girls don't get asked to dance." I knew what Janell meant and I remember her sincerity as she spoke, she believed it so intently, and at that moment, so would I.

A few years later, my all-girls high school was preparing for their annual winter formal, where the young women asked young men from different schools to be their dates. I remember a friend stopping by the house one afternoon and asking me if I had a date for the winter formal. "Not yet," I responded. My sister listened as my friend described a young man she knew, who may be available. She described this young man in a joking manner and continued to describe someone very rude, very reserved, and seemingly unfriendly. I thanked her for the suggestion and told her I would let her know if I needed the introduction.

When she left, Janell, again in all her wisdom, pulled me aside and said, "You are too amazing to settle for just anyone. Do not set your standards low. The right guy will be lucky to be with you, don't forget that!" Janell was right, I found a wonderful date for that dance and the ones after. I learned to believe in myself and my value, and to set my goals high.

Years later, I remember the day I introduced my sister to a bright-eyed blonde surfer from California, named Keith McCloskey. After meeting him for five minutes, Janell looked at my mom and whispered, "Get to know him, that man will be your future son-in-law!" Again, Janell was right.

Chapter 17

Just Show Up

"As we express our gratitude, we must never forget that the highest appreciation is not to utter words, but to live by them." John F. Kennedy

I was a freshman in high school, when the dentist decided I needed braces. Coincidentally, he applied them to my teeth right before my school's upcoming formal dance. The day after I received the braces, my boyfriend broke up with me, leaving me dateless for the big school dance. I arrived at school the next day, embarrassed and feeling unattractive. I was very quiet in my pain and walked the halls in silence, not even wanting to speak to my friends. "Jen, what's going on?" a good friend asked, plopping down next to me at our lunch table.

"You haven't opened your mouth once today. That's not like you," said a second friend, as she too moved to sit near me with her lunch. I slowly opened my mouth to reveal the metal covering on my teeth. I reluctantly showed them my braces and told them about the breakup, trying to fight back the hot, wet tears stinging my eyes. They tried to offer kind words of encouragement.

"They're not that bad. You can hardly notice them."

"Braces are kinda cool."

"He's a jerk, you don't need a guy who would break up with you because of a little metal in your mouth."

Nothing they said could console me. I allowed a single tear to fall quietly down my cheek as they spoke. I tried to remain stoic, but I was miserable on the inside.

What I remember most from that day was Teresa Troha. Teresa walked with me to my classes, sat next to me in every class we shared, and said nothing. She was just there. I remember to this day how much I appreciated her quiet comfort. She just showed up. I knew she was there if I needed to talk, even though I couldn't bring myself to say much. I just needed someone to be there, and she was. I don't think I spoke at all that afternoon, for fear of opening the flood gates.

Teresa was a shining example to me of what it means to just show up. Even when you don't know what to say or what to do, just being there is enough. I remember her actions to this day, and I try to be like Teresa; there for others, quietly, calmly, and caring. My dad always said, ninety percent of life is just showing up; so very true.

In 2016, I unexpectedly lost my oldest brother. As I walked into the church for his funeral, I looked up and was not surprised to see Teresa, my friend from high school, matching my stride. Although we hadn't spoken in years, she was there again, by my side, simply and quietly there for me.

Just show up. It's everything.

Chapter 18

Understanding is the Key

"Change your thoughts and you change your world."
Norman Vincent Peale

My parents didn't allow any of their children to obtain a driver's license until we turned seventeen years of age. The legal driving age in our state was sixteen, and all my friends received their licenses within days of their sixteenth birthday. I complained about the house rules vehemently to my brother Mike. "It's a rip-off and it's not fair. Why should we have to wait? All of my classmates have their driver's licenses, and some of them are younger than I am. I feel foolish having to ask them for rides, don't our parents trust me?" I inquired.

Mike stopped me in my tracks. "First, don't use those words. Be careful about the words you use, they actually describe yourself. Use confident words because you're a confident person. Always show people who you are by your words," he noted in a measured tone.

Then, he told me a story I had never heard before; one that allowed me to understand why my parents made this decision for their children. Understanding is the key. "Our grandmother, Dad's mom, was walking to the market very early one Sunday morning before church. She was on her way to buy the food she needed to prepare breakfast for her husband and nine children. She stepped off a curb and was hit by a sixteen-year-old drunk driver careening around a corner in his father's car. The young man was coming home from his prom. He was going so fast, he didn't see our grandmother. She was killed instantly. Dad was the second youngest of his siblings, and after the accident, all he heard growing up was a sixteen-years old is too young to be driving, too young to be responsible for a vehicle. Dad is not trying to take away your freedom. He is trying to allow you time to mature and grow before taking your life, and possibly the lives of others, into your own hands. He's protecting you. It is not about trust, it's about love."

I never questioned my father and the driving rules again. In a matter of minutes, I went from feeling cheated, to feeling honored and cared for, and received a lesson in understanding, love, and maturity.

Chapter 19

My Hero

"Perfection is not attainable, but if we chase perfection, we can catch excellence." Vince Lombardi

My father was the vice president of a large company. One day, during a weekly meeting, a team member, Clark, quite suddenly, collapsed. Jumping into action, my father immediately began CPR, and instructed the others to call for help. Rescue workers arrived and began emergency treatment, but it was obvious Clark was in a dire condition. They rushed him to a local hospital where, sadly, he died a few hours later.

My father came home that night completely deflated. He told my mother how he had failed in his attempt to save this man, and he was beside himself feeling the weight of what he considered to be an utter defeat.

As my mother attempted to console him, there was a knock on our front door. Surprisingly, it was Clark's family; his wife and two adult children. My father began apologizing for not being able to save their husband and father. Clark's son stopped my dad in his speech.

"You don't understand. We came to thank you. If it wasn't for your quick response and actions, my father would have died in that meeting room. Instead, we were able to be with him for his last few hours and say goodbye. What a difference it made to be able to talk to my dad. It's a conversation I will never forget, and I can't thank you enough."

I sat in the next room and listened intently to the discussion between my father and the man's family. It's a conversation I, too, will never forget. My father may not have saved his coworker that day, but he was still a hero, and this time, not just my hero.

You never know when you will have the opportunity to be someone's hero. It may not be something big, it might just be something small, but whenever you can, step up.

Seize the day.

Chapter 20

The Wooden Bunny

"Better to remain silent and be thought a fool than to speak out and remove all doubt." Abraham Lincoln

My dad loved to "tinker," in his garage, fixing things that once might have been thought to be useless. He enjoyed the art of finding more efficient ways to perform difficult tasks, and he loved organizing his tools, hardware, nails, screws, and bolts, most of which he kept in lidless mason jars.

One day, he brought me into the garage to see a wooden bunny he had created on his jigsaw. He replicated it after one he has purchased from a local craft fair. He had sanded the wood and painted it just like the bunny from the fair and had coated it with varnish to make it shine. Being young, I didn't realize the importance of what was about to transpire over the next few minutes. Dad showed me how he was able to carefully cut the bunny from a plain piece of wood and how he had attempted to match the professionally crafted bunny, perfectly. He explained the method he used to paint the bunny, and how he had even included a ribbon for its neck, just like the original. He was so proud of his work, I didn't realize he had found a new talent and would likely craft many more bunnies for the family. "Which of the two bunnies would you like to have?" He asked me, smiling.

To this day, I regret my response. I answered the way a child would, yet I find little solace in this fact. "I'll take the original bunny." The original was perfect, the paint was done with exact precision, the ribbon was bright, and the bunny face was very realistic. *Dad's is great, just not quite as perfect, I want the perfect one,* I remember thinking.

Dad handed me the original bunny, smiling, "Here you go, honey," he said without the slightest hint of remorse. But he never made another wooden bunny.

Looking back, I think my actions took the wind out of his sails. Years later, after my father had died and I had matured quite a bit, I found the original bunny in a box. In that moment, I realized that I would give anything to have the bunny my dad had crafted that day in our garage. The original bunny just looked cold and sterile with no character, no life, no twisted ribbon or glamorous paint job.

I searched for my dad's bunny, but never found it. Even today, the original sterile bunny sits on my dresser, not because I like it, but as a reminder to love what those around me make and do for me, even in their imperfections. I've learned that it's the imperfections that make those things perfect.

Chapter 21

What if I Fail?

"I have not failed. I've just found 10,000 ways that won't work." Thomas A. Edison

My brother, Mike, being a financial advisor and a genius in the world of investments, would often meet with older clients to discuss their financial portfolios. I remember Mike noting that so many of his older and seasoned clients would reiterate the same thoughts on life. They often reminded him of two life lessons. First, if they had known they were going to live this long, they would have taken better care of their bodies; and second, they wished they had fewer regrets in life. Regrets, not for things they did, but for things they didn't do. My mom and dad were living examples of this mentality.

I can remember as a child, I would be anxious about trying out for something for fear that I might not perform well. "What if I mess up?" I would whisper to my dad.

"What if you don't?" Dad would smile back.

67

To this day, when a negative thought tries to take over my mind, and I start to believe I can't do something or accomplish a goal, I remind myself, "What if I don't mess up? Imagine the possibilities."

Chapter 22

Class Act

"My father said there were two kinds of people in the world: givers and takers. The takers may eat better, but the givers sleep better." Marlo Thomas

My brother, Jim, was the quarterback on his high school football team. His high school was playing for a place in the state championship, and the team they were playing against was amazing. The opposing team had an injured player who remained in the game despite his injury, and was playing defense on the left side of the line. Jim's teammates recognized the situation and immediately thought to take advantage of the opportunity. Jim's head coach addressed my brother and whispered to him, "No matter what plays you call tonight, do not run or throw left," he directed. "If we beat them, we beat them at their best, not because we went against their weak and injured player. Trust me, the victory will mean even more. We will leave no doubt in anyone's eyes that we won because we're the better team." Then he sent Jim onto the field to lead his team.

Jim did as he was directed, and with each play he avoided the opposing player on the left side. Jim's team won the game, and its place in the state's championship that year.

My brother recalls the meeting after the game which made the real impact on his life. As the teams were shaking hands and congratulating each other, the coach of the opposing team approached Jim and paused, he reached out his hand and said, "That was classy, young man, you played the game with class!"

Jim nodded as a lump rose in his throat. He realized he was receiving praise from his opponent, for a job well done. That lesson changed the way he lived his life, as he strived every day to make his actions those of class.

Chapter 23

I Wish I Could

"The future belongs to those who believe in the beauty of their dreams." Eleanor Roosevelt

When I was young, I remember watching a pilot on television fly his plane and maneuver it in such a way that it was inspirational. I watched in amazement, and after the show was over, I said with great excitement, "I wish I could do that!"

"Why don't you?" Dad replied.

"I don't know how to fly or where to start learning to fly," I responded meekly.

"So, pick up the phone!" Dad encouraged.

This was prior to computers and the internet. In his mind, making a phone call, and finding out what to do, was the best way to research. "There is no difference between that person and you, they just knew how to obtain the information they needed to get the job done. You have that ability, pick up the phone," he insisted.

I remember watching the Olympics with my mom and after watching each performance, Mom would pontificate, repeating the same phrase. "I bet you can do that!" I was young and a decent gymnast, but by no means could I slalom ski or pole vault. My mom was so confident that I could perform all those amazing skills, I started to believe it myself. She not only gave me confidence, but the belief that she knew I could do anything I set my mind on doing. To this day, I watch the Olympics and think, *I bet I could do that.* Thanks, Mom.

The mentality of, *find-a-way,* stays with me to this day. Anyone can tell you why something can't be done, I just need one way that it can be done. I will strive every day to find a way. My father taught me I could do anything, and my mother cheered for me the entire time I tried.

Chapter 24

Exploring

"The more you sweat in peace, the less you bleed in war."
Norman Schwarzkopf

My dad was also a realtor for many years, and before cell phones and Global Positioning Systems (GPS) in our cars, Dad studied maps, so he could learn the streets and their names. He always knew the quickest or most beautiful route to take a prospective client.

When I was young, my dad would say, "Hey, let's go exploring!" That meant long hours in the car, driving down roads to see where they led. Finding more no-through streets and dead-ends than I ever knew existed, Dad found joy in the smallest things. He often reminded me, "If you know your general direction, you can fly by the seat of your pants and find anything." He taught me how to read the sun to determine your general direction. There was a very old house, which had been converted into a small restaurant called, "The Happy Pickle," where we would often stop on exploration days, to have lunch. The only good thing about, "exploring," when I was young, was it either ended in lunch at the Happy Pickle or a Slurpee from 7-11. Dad was so thrilled when he found a shortcut or a new road no one knew about.

As I grew older, while on these excursions exploring the county, I remember thinking, *This is pointless, none of these roads mean anything to me. It feels like we are going in circles.* I realize now that I wasted the one-on-one time in the car with my dad. Looking back, I should have asked him to tell me stories of his childhood, asked him who his heroes were, or to teach me something new.

Not long after obtaining my driver's license, I was driving down the road with a friend, after we had dropped a schoolmate at her house. We had never been to this person's house before and had been taking the back roads while talking and laughing, not paying attention to the roads we were driving. We pulled out of her driveway and headed back to where we thought was home. We drove for what seemed like hours but came no closer to home; we were lost. Trying to find where we were, without a cell phone and GPS, seemed almost impossible. The sun started to set and neither of us wanted to admit we had lost our bearings. I looked at the setting sun and thankfully remembered my dad's advice about directions. Okay, we were heading north, that was correct, but everything looked so unfamiliar. We turned down a new road, hoping something would trigger our location and there, on a side street just over the hill, was a small house converted into a restaurant. The Happy Pickle stood like a beacon. I knew where we were.

Though it was years later, I had remembered this place and how to arrive home from its doorstep. Now, I welcome the new and exploring mindset. I will forever think of my father with every new discovery and silently thank him for the beautiful days when he took me exploring.

Chapter 25

The Balance Beam

"There is no disgrace in failure, the disgrace is not to try."
Cathy Rigby Mason

When I was a small child, I took gymnastic lessons at a local gym. One afternoon, the gym was having a sale to clear away a few old pieces of equipment they no longer needed. "How much for the old balance beam on the floor?" my father asked the owner.

"Just five dollars for that piece."

"Sold!" said Dad, and the money was exchanged.

Dad made a few slight modifications to the apparatus, and by the afternoon, I was twirling and spinning on my new balance beam to my heart's desire. This transaction started my daily balance beam addiction.

I continued my love of gymnastics for years. In college, at the University of Maryland, I participated on their gymnastic exhibition team. At the end of each season, our troupe held its annual *Home Show,* where our family and friends could attend our season's final exhibition. My favorite event was, of course, the balance beam. I had many years of practice, and with much excitement, I mounted the beam. For some reason that night, my first pass was slightly off, and I fell off the beam. My confidence didn't wane, and without a thought, I jumped back on and continued. A leap, a turn, a back walkover and again a fall. I hopped back on quickly and continued with another skill, falling yet again. I jumped back on immediately, almost hoping no one noticed. Right before my dismount, I fell again. This routine looked more like a trampoline exercise than a balance beam routine. Once more, I hopped back onto the beam, completed the routine and dismounted. I fell off the beam a disheartening four times that night, but I completed the show, performing other events with my head held high, even though my heart was low.

When the entire performance was over, our troupe spilled into the audience to be congratulated. Everyone commented on how wonderful the show was and how we all performed so beautifully. No one said anything about my bouncing balance beam routine. Once the crowd had thinned, I noticed my father standing in the back of the Field House. I walked up to him, trying not to show my embarrassment.

"I learned something about you tonight," he said softly with a slight grin. "You're not a quitter," he said proudly, as he reached out and hugged me. I remember hugging him back, tightening my hold as the silent tears ran down my cheek and onto his chest. I was crying, not because of his compassion, but because of his ability to see the light in the darkest situation and I was so grateful he was my father. He learned something about me that night, but I learned something about life, and more importantly, about myself. I have never forgotten those words. They made me who I am today.

Chapter 26

The Tug-of-War

"Nothing is impossible, the word itself says 'I'm possible!'"
Audrey Hepburn

One Saturday, while in college at the University of Maryland, we held a sort of *College Dormitory Olympics*. My dad surprised me and attended our event. The typical college Olympic Games were played, and Dad cheered for me and my dorm-mates during every crazy challenge. I checked in with Dad between events, to be sure he was enjoying himself and not feeling ignored. He loved being surrounded by the young adults and was having the time of his life watching our maneuvers. The big Olympics finale was a tug-of-war between the two leading teams. To make the event even more exciting, the University of Maryland Fire Department brought their suds machine to the event. The goal was to provide a foam and mud pit for the tug-of-war losers to fall into immersing them in muck and suds, while instantly glorifying the winners.

It was time for the last event, and my team was one of the finalists. We watched and waited while the fire department crew attempted to start the massive suds machine. This seemed to be taking an unusual amount of time. I glanced over at my dad, who had been standing a few yards away from the machine, watching the fire crew intently. I ran over to check on him. "What seems to be the issue over there, Jen?" He inquisitively asked.

"Looks like the crew is having a little trouble getting their suds machine started," I began. But before I had finished my sentence, my father handed me his sports coat, rolled up his sleeves, and in a few strides, he was talking to the firefighters. I turned around to see my father had one foot up on the suds machine engine and the firefighters were handing him tools. Everyone kept asking me, "Who is that man?" To which I replied proudly, "That's my dad!"

Needless to say, my dad repaired the suds machine that day and the engine started up, with a loud cheer from the awaiting participants. Unfortunately, my team lost the tug of war that day, and as I was covered in mud and suds, somehow, it didn't matter. What mattered was my dad saved the day. My dad, the man who taught me to never give up and to always try.

Chapter 27

The Greatest Revenge

"I will love the light for it shows me the way, yet I will endure the darkness, because it shows me the stars." Og Mandino

One evening, I was sitting in my apartment, quietly, when my sister, Janell, called. Right away, she noticed my voice was slightly off and she inquired why. I could hear the loud and boisterous voices of her young boys, Josh and Sam, in the background and not wanting to burden her, I insisted I was fine. She continued to press for an answer. "I know you, you are not fine, something is up. What's wrong Jen?" she whispered. Janell knew me better than anyone, her caring attitude always made me feel so loved. We were not just sisters, we were friends. We could share anything, she was always there for me.

I confessed I was very upset about my recent break-up with my boyfriend. I tried to reassure her I was okay, and I reminded her and myself, I didn't need to love someone who didn't love me back.

As she listened to me trying to be brave that night, she ended our phone call with some of the best advice I had ever received. She whispered, "You know Jen, the best revenge, is to live well." I knew I would move on to bigger and better things in my life, better relationships, and happier times. I've always remembered this advice, not because I wanted revenge or to show anyone I could survive, or be better than anyone else, but to remind me there was something greater and I would no doubt find it. Think well of yourself. Treat yourself with kindness and do the things that make you happy and live well. Thank you, Janell, for preparing my heart for the future.

Chapter 28

From the Window

"How wonderful it is that nobody need wait a single moment before starting to improve the world." Anne Frank

Our neighbor, Ms. Ann, died very young. She was survived by a wonderful husband and four amazing young daughters. The young women all grew up right across the street from our house and we watched as they lived very full and meaningful lives, despite losing their mom so early in life. I remember seeing how much my mom and dad took their loss to heart. They would send food over to the family, frequently, always thinking of them and looking out for their best interests. I would often find Mom sitting on our front porch talking to one of the young ladies about school, friends, and life. Mom kept a watchful eye on the young women as they grew. Their father was amazing, but Mom felt a need to protect them, like a surrogate Mother.

One evening, one of the daughters, Liz, had been dropped off at the house by her boyfriend. Mom knew Liz's boyfriend, Alex, and watched as he pulled into the driveway and allowed Liz to walk alone toward her dark house. Mom happened to be walking past her bedroom window when Alex and Liz pulled into the driveway that night. I remember the window flying open and Mom, calling to Alex, "You get out of that car and walk her to the door like a gentleman. The house is dark! Don't you ever let me catch you just dropping her off without walking her to the door like that again." Alex quickly emerged from the car and Liz graciously accepted the escort for the five steps into her house. I was so embarrassed as Mom shouted out the window at poor Alex.

The next day, Liz was at our door. Mom welcomed her in and apologized for her outburst. "Don't apologize, I came to thank you," said Liz. Liz was thrilled to know Mom was keeping Alex on his toes and she thanked Mom for intervening.

Alex and Liz were married shortly after and they now have two amazing daughters, who are, no doubt, escorted to their house at the end of their dates, also.

Chapter 29

Make it Right

"Sometimes you make the right decision, sometimes you make the decision right." Phil McGraw

I was offered an exciting new job opportunity and I was having a tough time making the decision, to take the offer, or stay with my current job. I called Dad to ask his advice. I always wanted his thoughts on tough decisions. I told him of my loyalty to my current job and how I absolutely loved the people, but the new job offered an exciting fresh challenge.

Dad listened as I methodically addressed the pros and cons of each position. He listened as I explained the benefits of each career. After I had spoken for quite a while, I asked Dad what he thought. His opinion meant the world to me. I knew he would help me make the right decision.

"It sounds like you have already made your decision." He chuckled.

"Not really, I am not sure," I persisted.

"Jen, just remember, any decision you make is right because you'll make it right," he reminded me. "If you stay at your current position, you'll be happy. You will love the people you work with and continue to grow, I have no doubt. If you take the new position, you will meet new people, learn the job and continue to grow. Whatever decision you make, you will make it right, so there's no need to worry."

Those words guide me to this day. Have confidence in yourself and your decisions.

Chapter 30

Tips

"Preach the gospel, and if necessary, use words." St Francis of Assisi

I was preparing to train salespeople for a seminar I was to give the following week and I shared with my mom the research and interviews I had done to prepare. Mom, being a realtor for forty years said, "I have a few tips for you."

"Sure," I said, eagerly remembering that she had been in the million-dollar sales club for many of those forty years. "What are your thoughts?"

"Whenever I spoke with potential clients and visited them at their home, to offer to list their property and place it on the market through my company, I remembered four critical things." Mom grinned. "Wipe your feet before you walk in the door, showing you care about their home. Shake their hand, firm thumb to thumb while looking them in the eye and smiling, showing you are excited to meet them. If they have a baby, kiss it, and a dog, pet it! Show interest in them, let them know they are important, not just because they are a potential client, but because they are a potential friend."

Mom reminded me that *respect* was the pillar upon which to build your clientele. My mom not only had repeat customers, but because of her caring approach and her length of time in the business, she was the realtor for many of her early client's children, looking for their first home and a new friend.

Chapter 31

Young Jim

"A true conservationist is a man who knows that the world is not given by his fathers, but borrowed from his children."
John James Audubon

I was babysitting for my nephew, Jim, when he was three-years old. His family had a unique computer and my three-year-old nephew knew how it worked and how to play his favorite computer games. His father had shown him how to log on and how to select the correct games. On this particular evening, I indulged him, and we played computer games together for many hours. Suddenly, in the middle of a game, the computer screen went black. My nephew made his three-year-old attempt to repair the system, but to no avail. I tried to regain the display screen, but nothing seemed to work. I immediately engaged him in another activity, to distract him, and perhaps me, from the fact that we had just broken their expensive family computer.

Like all three-year-olds, Jim wanted to stay awake until his parents arrived home. I obliged, hoping no mention would be made to the earlier malfunctioning computer when they arrived home. Jim and I played board games and read books and soon, the computer was forgotten.

The instant my brother and his wife walked in the door, my nephew jumped to his feet, took his father's hand and walked him over to the blank computer screen. "Look, Daddy, it stopped working!" he said. I immediately began struggling to provide a possible excuse as to how this may have occurred. Before I could come up with a reason why I was not at fault, my brother hit a few keys and the computer was up and running again. My brother praised his son for bringing the issue to his attention.

My little nephew reminded me to face my fears, to be honest and forthright. A three-year-old taught me a unique lesson in character that day.

Chapter 32

The Stranger

"The deeper that sorrow carves into your being, the more joy you can contain." Kahlil Gibran

My father was diagnosed with terminal stomach cancer three and a half weeks before my wedding. When my mother, siblings, and I came home to my parents' house from the hospital the day of the diagnosis, we were crying and attempting as best we could to comfort each other. My parents had a construction worker at their home fine-tuning some wallpaper and paint, prior to the wedding. The young man, who was working on my parents' hallway at the time, watched as we all walked in crying and holding on to one another.

Realizing what this must look like to someone who had no idea what was happening, I approached him and said, "I'm so sorry for all the turmoil in the house. We've just gotten some very bad news."

The young man looked at me and said, "I don't know what you are going through right now, but I want you to know, it is all going to be okay."

It was as if those words just rang in my head, it will be okay—it will be okay. For some reason, I clung to those words. The young wallpaper man packed up his tools and left shortly after. My family and I continued to cry, and comfort, and talk about what to do next. The entire time those words echoed in my mind. It will be okay. At that moment, I felt peace. Those kind words from a stranger helped me throughout the time of my father's illness. Just knowing there was hope, and kind words to offer sympathy, made a difference.

Be the difference.

Chapter 33

Amy

"We get strength and encouragement from watching children." Hayao Miyazaki

The day of my wedding to Keith, my father was getting dressed in his tuxedo. Having gone through stomach cancer surgery three weeks before, he had a significant incision on his abdomen. As he dressed, his incision started to open and began bleeding. Careful not to bleed on his shirt, he immediately tried to repair the wound. My godmother, Rosalie, was dressing for my wedding at my parents' house that day, and being a nurse, she immediately butterfly stitched my dad's bleeding incision.

He walked me down the aisle that evening, with braces on his legs under his tuxedo pants, and bleeding from his open wound. Somehow, he stayed very positive, smiling broadly all throughout the evening as he shared in my excitement. I had no idea he was in pain until the Father-Daughter dance.

Right before the Father-Daughter dance, I remember seeing my nieces, Jenny and Erin, and my nephews, Jimmy and Chris. They were all in our wedding party and all very young. They took turns dancing with our two-year-old flower girl, their youngest sister Amy. They tried desperately to keep her off the dance floor, while the DJ prepared for his announcement of the Father-Daughter Dance. Erin and Jenny tried to coax Amy to dance with them off to the side of the dance floor, but Amy had other plans.

Before our dance, Dad asked if I could have the DJ shorten the song we were planning to dance to because he worried his legs could not endure. I asked the DJ to cut the song short; however, the DJ had no idea that everyone at my wedding knew my father had terminal cancer. Most of them knew his days were numbered, so all of the attendees circled the dance floor to take pictures of me and my dad, many attendees knowing it would be the last time they would ever see him. Seeing the crowd of people, the DJ continued the lengthy Father-Daughter dance song, despite my request.

I could tell my dad was uncomfortable, and I asked him if he wanted to stop. "I'll be okay," he continued in his stoic and loving way. We danced to the Bette Midler song, *Wind Beneath My Wings*. As the words rang out, I thought how my dad was indeed my hero, as he continued to dance with me and for me, not wanting to cut our Father-Daughter Dance short.

How can we stop without bringing attention to my dad? I thought. I raised my eyes to Heaven and asked for a miracle, before my dad's legs started to stumble. Just then, my flower-girl Amy, barely two years old, wandered onto the dance floor. She walked up to us as we danced, and pulled on Pop-pop's leg.

"Hi Pop-pop," she mumbled. My dad stopped dancing and looked down at the little angel dressed in purple and pearls.

"Hi Amy," he swooned, smiling and reaching for her.

Everyone immediately focused on Amy and my dad's tenderness with her. Her persistence allowed us to stop dancing and move to the edge of the dance floor, where my dad could take a seat. I knew we had been given a gift. My father honored me by dancing the Father-Daughter dance with me, and Amy gave him the gift of slowing down, so he could finish with style.

I am forever grateful to my father, who danced with me that night and to a little angel dressed in purple, who was wise enough to jump in and dance with us.

Chapter 34

3-2-1

"Darkness cannot drive out darkness; only light can do that. Hate cannot drive out hate; only love can do that."
Martin Luther King, Jr.

One evening, Keith and I had heard my friend, Ursula, speak about the power of love. She noted that there may be times in a relationship when saying, "I love you," might be difficult. She emphasized the importance of making sure your loved ones felt loved, even though the words may not be available. She shared with us a method she and her husband, Larry, used when words were not enough or unavailable. She shared with us how they had experienced a difficult loss, and neither of them wanted to talk.

They had derived a method to share their, "I love you's," when words were too difficult. Ursula described how she would squeeze Larry's hand three times, as if to say, "I love you." A squeeze for each word. Larry immediately knew what she was thinking and squeezed her hand back twice denoting, without words, "Love-you." She would squeeze back one squeeze denoting, "Thanks!"

Keith and I loved this idea, and often when we were holding hands, we would exchange the alternating three squeeze, two squeeze, one squeeze, to remind each other we were there, and we loved each other. We even used the method if we were driving behind each other, on the road. When Keith was driving in front of me, he would tap his brakes three times, flashing his brake lights for me to see. I would respond by flashing my car's brights twice, and he would tap his brakes once, flashing the brake lights in a specific pattern, and only we knew the beautiful code.

My dad had been in the hospital for a few weeks with symptoms from his stomach cancer, and was there over the Fourth of July. Keith and I decided to by-pass the fireworks and spend the evening with Dad, in his hospital room, watching the fireworks on his little hospital TV. We shared with Dad how we were having so much fun with our new found *I love you* code. Dad appreciated the ingenuity of the code and laughed as we shared its many applications. We stayed with my dad until very late that night, making sure he was not alone. We talked about our favorite movies and about anything Dad had on his mind. I was grateful to Keith for embracing the opportunity to spend time with my dad.

As Keith and I left the hospital that night, I remember looking at the hospital windows and counting the floors. I was wondering which window was my dad's. As we climbed into the car that night, I was already missing my dad. In a crazy attempt to send a message to him, I looked at the solemn hospital building, and even though it was very late, I honked my horn three times, just in case my Dad was listening, and just in case he remembered the code, and just in case he needed to know I loved him. Much to my surprise, a light on Dad's floor came on and flickered twice. Not only had he remembered the code, he was waiting to respond. Feeling connected to my dad from the parking lot, I honked back once to let him know, I was so very thankful for him and his willingness to connect even when words were not available.

Chapter 35

Thumb-less

"The best way to find yourself is to lose yourself in the service of others." Mahatma Gandhi

My father was in the middle of his fight against stomach cancer and his long battle. I was with him the day the doctors inserted a feeding tube, directly into his stomach. He seemed to be in pain after the tube was inserted, so I peeked to see where it was attached, and realized the new feeding tube was not properly secured. When I called this to the attention of my father's surgeon, he indirectly tried to tell me it was the best they could do at this time. He was trying to say, however indirectly, that my father's time was limited.

Still not obtaining the response I needed, I said sharply, "If it was your father, would you let that tube remain loose like this, knowing he was in pain?" I lifted the sheet to display the loose insertion.

Without another word, the orderlies were summoned to wheel my father back into the procedure room. I was angry, and frustrated, and wanted to cry, but I held back my tears. *I haven't given up on him, neither should they,* I thought as I hurried alongside his bed, while they wheeled him back into the procedure room.

I parked myself on the floor outside the procedure room, since there were no chairs in this hallway. I sat there, knees tucked up to my chest, head down in prayer, hoping for a miracle. Eventually, I lifted my chin and saw a gentleman sitting on the floor, leaning against the wall, on the opposite side of the hall from me. His hand was wrapped with thick gauze. Being the only two people in the hallway, I asked him, "Are you okay?"

"Yeah, just waiting for the doctor. A chair would be nice." He laughed wryly and I nodded my head in agreement.

"What happened to your hand?" I asked, trying to be polite.

"Well, I work construction and I was reaching for something and got it caught between two girders. I ripped my darn thumb right off," he answered very calmly, almost in disbelief.

"I am so sorry, are you in pain? Can they reattach it?" I asked sympathetically.

"No," he answered very calmly again. "There is nothing there. I really don't have much pain."

We talked for a while about his bravery, and his calmness. We even laughed about how he casually described the injury. I expressed how sorry I was for him, and he assured me he would be fine. For a brief moment, I was lost in his story, forgetting my sadness and heartache.

"Why are you here?" he asked, snapping me back to reality. In that split second, I realized my father was behind that door and I could do nothing to help him. "My father has cancer," was all I could manage to get out.

"Oh, my goodness, I am so sorry!" he said. "Please forgive me for going on about my injury, while your dad is going through that kind of pain, I am so sorry!" he said graciously, nearing embarrassment.

His kindness and appreciation of my father, and his situation, allowed my tears to escape. Almost on cue, my father was wheeled out of the procedure room. Quickly wiping my eyes, I jumped up and said, "Hi Daddy." The gentleman on the floor used his uninjured hand and pushed up the corners of his lips reminding me to smile in front of my dad. I nodded my head in acknowledgement. With one hand, I grabbed my father's hand and placed my other hand on the man's shoulder, as we passed by him. "Bless you," I said quietly. He just nodded and smiled.

Dad and I went back to his room where the nurses continued to monitor him. In honor of the man in the hall, I told my dad funny stories to keep his spirits high. I have never forgotten that man, and I hope somehow, he reads this. I hope he knows that in 1992, in a Bethesda Hospital hallway, he made a difference.

Chapter 36

Not Afraid

"Better to light one candle than to curse the darkness."
Chinese proverb

My father had been in and out of the hospital while fighting cancer. He had been told there was nothing the doctors could do, and they gave him three months to live. Dad lived nine months beyond their expectations. With his family by his side, he fought for treatment and for life, every single day. He believed attitude was the key and he lived vivaciously every moment.

One very quiet and calm afternoon, I entered his hospital room. The room was dark, the shades were drawn, and the television was off. I entered to see my dad lying on his side with his eyes open almost in a trance. His usual grand greeting gave way to a motionless gaze.

"Hi, Pop," I said softly, "Are you okay?"

"I am," he said still gazing into the darkness of the room.

"Dad, I am worried about you. I feel a little like you are giving up," I whispered softly.

Dad replied gently, "I never said I was giving up, I'm just not afraid to die."

We both sat in the quiet dark room pondering those words. I didn't bother to wipe the tears that fell from my eyes. I just let them fall silently. I knew he had made his peace with the situation.

"God needs a good cabinet maker in heaven," he said finally.

God now has the best.

Chapter 37

The Battery

"Be miserable. Or motivate yourself. Whatever has to be done, it's always your choice." Wayne Dyer

My brother, Mike, has always inspired me. He has taught me so much about life and laughter. One day, I was visiting my brother's office, where he worked as a senior investment counselor. On his desk sat a large battery. "Mike, why is this odd thing sitting on your otherwise meticulously clean desk?" I teased.

"You see Jen, I keep this battery as a reminder. In life, some people will drain your battery, and some will charge your battery. It reminds me to surround myself with people who charge my battery, and to be someone who charges others."

"Makes sense," I replied.

"Always surround yourself with people who charge your battery and avoid the ones who drain it," Mike reiterated.

"Which am I?" I asked.

"You're still here," he replied.

Chapter 38

Little Did I Know

"The value of a man should be seen in what he gives and not in what he is able to receive." Albert Einstein

When I was in high school, I sat next to Erin Tehan in math class. Erin was sweet, and kind, and full of life. We were friends; however, I had no idea the young woman sitting next to me, would have such a significant impact later in my life. Erin and I went to different colleges, after graduation. We would see each other at yearly high school gatherings, converse a little and catch up, but little else. I had no idea that when my father was admitted to the hospital, Erin would be his oncology nurse.

Erin was different from the other nurses, and because she knew me from high school, she would take a little extra time with my dad. I would find them laughing and talking when I came to visit, and I quickly realized that my dad's spirit seemed to be dependent on Erin's shifts. At the end of a long hospital visit, Erin was checking with Dad's doctor to ensure he could return home. Erin had been talking to Dad and she learned about his afternoon plans once he was discharged. She listened while he spoke about his hammock, and the birds in his back yard. She listened as he shared his excitement to eat watermelon on the patio.

The oncologist informed Erin that my father's blood pressure was too high and he had a slight temperature, and therefore, would not be discharged. Erin knew keeping him any longer in the hospital would worsen these symptoms. She addressed Dad's oncologist, explaining how a hammock was waiting for Dad, and the watermelon was ripe and ready to be cut. She explained, in detail, what going home meant to her patient. Her persistent requests continued, until she won her case. Dad was finally released and sent home. An hour after Dad arrived home, his blood pressure was back to normal and his fever dropped.

Two months later, Dad returned to the hospital in the middle of the night, via ambulance. Our family was notified in the early morning, and we dressed and headed to the hospital. My mom was on her way, and since I lived closest to the hospital, I was the first to arrive. Knowing Dad was likely worried and alone, I rushed to his bedside. There, sitting in Dad's room, with her legs comfortably crisscrossed in the chair, was Erin, chatting amicably with Dad. He was thrilled she was working that evening/early morning and so was I. Dad told me she had been there when he arrived, and he felt so much better knowing she was taking care of him.

Erin stayed in our room and went over Dad's information with me thoroughly. I asked every question I had, and after a while, I realized I had monopolized much of her time. "Erin, go be with your other patients, I know Dad and I have taken so much of your time already," I urged.

"No worries," Erin whispered as she headed for the door, "I have been off duty for hours."

Later that month, on a cold September morning, it was Erin's hand I felt on my shoulder when my mother, siblings, and I prayed over my father's body, when Dad went to meet his maker. Little did I know, the young woman in math class would later be my hero.

Chapter 39

Sentimental Journey

"Every day is a journey, and the journey itself is home."
Matsuo Basho

My father was pronounced dead on September 23, 1992, at 7:05 a.m., of stomach cancer. With time having been very limited for my dad, my family had spent as much time as we could with him, before we lost him to this disease. Even when the doctors told, us in early February, that Dad was on borrowed time, he continued, he never stopped living his life. We began to think, somehow, he would just keep going, even after months in the hospital. My mom was with him on the morning of September 23rd. None of his family had expected him to die that morning. My mom spent the night in his hospital room, and she sang to him all night. "What did you sing?" her inquisitive children asked.

"Sentimental Journey and all of the songs we would sing on our road trips in the car," Mom informed us.

Dad quietly slipped away and took his sentimental journey home, to meet his maker, that morning. The song, *Sentimental Journey,* became our mantra for the next few days. As we prepared for his funeral, we would hum and sing it throughout Mom's house, as if to suggest Dad was on a new journey. My husband, Keith, and I stayed with Mom that week. The beauty of that song came to light the morning of his funeral. I was singing the song out loud, as we were dressing for the service, when the words of the song struck me. I ran into my mom's room and said excitedly, "Sing the words, sing the words!"

She began, "*Gonna take a Sentimental Journey,*

Gonna set my heart at ease,

Gonna make a sentimental journey,

To renew old memories.

I've got my bag and got my reservation,

Spent each dime I could afford.

Like a child in wild anticipation,

Long to hear that, 'all aboard!'

Seven, (seven)

That's the time we leave,

At seven (seven)

I'll be waiting out for heaven, (heaven)..."

Mom gasped. Seven, my dad died at 7:00 o'clock. He was pronounced dead at 7:05, but we all know Dad died at exactly 7 a.m., just like the words in the song. Even in his dying, he was right on time.

"...Counting every mile of railroad track

That takes me back,

Never thought my heart could be so yearning,

Why did I decide to roam?

Got to take this sentimental journey,

Sentimental journey home.

Seven, That's the time we leave,

At seven,

I'll be waiting out for heaven,

Counting every mile of railroad track

That takes me back."

Chapter 40

Comfortable Shoes

"Peace is not the absence of trouble, but the presence of Christ." Sheila Walsh

The morning after my father passed, my mom sent my husband, Keith, and me to the funeral home with specific instructions, "Give the funeral home director Dad's favorite blue suit and his beautiful dress shoes, but in the coffin have them put his favorite and most comfortable slippers," she said as she gently handed them to me.

I thought, perhaps, since Dad died of cancer, his feet may have been swollen and his shoes might not fit properly, but I was curious as to the actual reason she wanted him to have both. When I presented the clothes and two pairs of shoes to the funeral director, he was not at all surprised. He nodded and said there would be no problem. When I returned home, I asked Mom why she had sent two pair of shoes for my father.

Whenever something unexplainable would happen, or an unpleasant event would occur, like when a child would become ill, my mom would always say, "Put comfortable

119

shoes in my coffin!" I always wondered what she meant. On this day she explained.

She had always believed when you die, you walk the *"last mile,"* with your maker and discuss with him the times you separated yourself from him. She believed you were accountable for those times, and in that *last mile* you were also shown the light and understanding of events from your past. Mom believed you could talk to God and ask him about events in your life, why people died, and even, why sometimes it appeared as if we were abandoned by God. She knew it was then, that you would gain a deeper understanding of God's plan. In her mind, she expected that my father may have to walk the *last mile,* and she wanted him to have the most comfortable shoes for his journey into paradise.

Mom has many questions for God and believes her walk will be long as a result. She has asked her children to place comfortable shoes in her coffin one day, and by doing so, we will be guaranteeing her a comfortable walk on her inquisitive and anticipated *last mile.* Sometimes things may not make sense to us now, but in God's time, she knows they will.

So, to my children, in the hopefully very far future, please, put comfortable shoes in my coffin, too.

Chapter 41

He No Longer Needs Them

"The only thing worse than being blind, is having sight but no vision." Helen Keller

My father wore glasses from the time he was a young boy. I rarely saw my dad without his glasses. When he slept, his glasses remained on the nightstand and he even put them on to read the clock, when he awoke. Shortly after my father's passing, I dreamed of him. The dream was so clear and so real I remember thinking, *I almost don't recognize you, Dad.* He looked young, healthy, and happy. I remember his face, the shirt he was wearing, and everything about the dream; it was so vivid. When I recalled the dream the next morning, explaining the details to my husband, Keith, I reiterated that I almost didn't recognize my dad. "He looked so strong and he wasn't even wearing his glasses."

Keith smiled and simply said, "He no longer needs them."

Chapter 42

The Three "C"s

"I do the 'New York Times' crossword puzzle every morning to keep the old grey matter ticking." Carol Burnett

Mom would always tell us, get dressed every morning, put on your lipstick, and comb your hair. After my father passed in 1992, we were hopeful Mom would continue this practice; thankfully, she did. Every day she takes a bath, puts on her lipstick, and brushes her hair. These little things have helped keep Mom in her daily routine, which has helped to keep her blood pressure in check.

The daily bath is her decompression time. She thinks and plans her day, while she soaks in her tub. She comes out refreshed and ready for the world. People often ask my mom, "How are you still alive at ninety-eight years old?" She corrects them by saying, "I am ninety-eight years young." To Mom, attitude is everything. She believes she can, so she can.

Dale Carnegie teaches to live by the three "C"s. Mom has adopted this mantra. "I make sure I never criticize, condemn, or complain," she says proudly. "Well, I try not to," she adds while smiling. My children, her other grandchildren, and her great-grandchildren witness her example and they too choose to live by the three "C"s. Mom believes you live by the three "C"s for others, not just yourself.

One afternoon, we went to renew Mom's driver's license and they asked her if she wanted to be an organ donor. "If I can do one last thing to help someone else, so be it," she replied. "Yes, sign me up," she replied cheerfully! She is always giving, always thinking of others.

Attitude is the backbone, the baseline, the foundation, from which everything else is measured. Mom always believes everything will be okay. "I am in greater hands than my own." Attitude means mind set and outlook. Our attitude is based on our experiences, our appreciation, and the lessons we take from these experiences. Everyone's experiences are different, yet everyone's attitude is a reflection of their personal resolution of the circumstances which surround them.

My father always said, "The pessimist curses the wind, the optimist, hopes the wind will change, and the realist adjusts her sails." My mother's attitude is not one of cursing, not one of wishing, but one of action, resulting in sheer delight.

Chapter 43

"Momma's Buying a Donkey"

"An honest man is always a child." Socrates

When my daughter was two, I gently shared with her that in a few months she was going to be a big sister. Without missing a beat, she said, "Okay mom, I guess you'll be going to Bethlehem."

At two years old, the only person she had ever learned about who had a baby, was a young woman named Mary, who had her child in a manger in Bethlehem, after a long journey on a donkey. She recalled the story of how Mary and Joseph looked for a room for the evening and how their baby was born that beautiful night. As I explained the difference in our stories, she was still convinced her baby sibling would be born in Bethlehem.

Later that month, I asked Mariah to share our exciting news with the extended family. It was no surprise to us all when she announced to the rest of the family, "My Momma's buying a donkey!"

Out of the mouths of babes!

Chapter 44

The Folded Paper

"Nearly all men can stand adversity, but if you want to test a man's character, give him power." Abraham Lincoln

My brother, Mike, is an amazing investment counselor, with a brilliant reputation. Recently, a competitor contacted him about working for their firm. Mike was content in his current organization, but agreed to discuss the potential opportunity with the competitor. He was given a tour of the competitor's large and pristine office, and was then taken to a room of senior executives sitting around a large conference table. The executive team shared with Mike about the firm's success and about their benefits and bonus structure. In a grand attempt to entice Mike, the senior most executive said, "We are prepared to give you a large bonus to join our team." He then slid a folded piece of paper in front of Mike.

"Let me understand this correctly," Mike said questioning. "On this piece of paper is the amount you will pay me to come to your firm."

"Yes," the senior executive said proudly and boastfully, as if knowing the number would impress Mike.

Mike put his hand on the paper and closed his eyes for a moment in thought. "If I come to work for your company, it will be because it is in the best interest of my clients, not for me. I don't want to make this decision because of what's on this paper, I would like to make it based on stability and potential for my clients," Mike responded. Calmly, he slid the folded paper back to the senior executive, without opening it.

His actions that day reminded me of the true definition of love, putting someone else's needs before your own.

Chapter 45

Lemme-Go

"There are only two lasting bequests we can hope to give our children. One of these is roots, the other, wings."
Johann Wolfgang von Goethe

On Saturday mornings, when my daughter Mariah was very young, I would take her to swim lessons. My younger son, Trey, accompanied me in his diaper and pajamas. Being very young and inquisitive, he always tried to run toward the water. I would hold him intently as we watched and cheered for his sister, who was brilliantly learning to kick her legs and stroke the water with her arms.

Each week we watched, and each week, my son desperately tried to jump into the swimming pool. Often, at the end of Mariah's sessions, we would remove Trey's shoes and allow him to sit in my lap and hang his feet in the pool. He splashed intently and it was clear he was dreaming of the day he too, would be swimming like his sister.

My daughter's instructor noted Trey's excitement and said, "Why don't you bring your suit next week and bring him into the pool after Mariah's lesson?"

The next week, after Mariah's lesson, with Trey on my hip, I stepped into the water. Trey immediately tried to push me away, and with his limited verbal ability, at his young age blurted out, "Lemme-go, lemme-go!" He continued this while pushing me away. "Lemme–go," his young voice persisted, as he squirmed continuously. I thought, *If I let you go, you will drown, no way.* But as he persisted, I quieted my nerves and gently gave way to his request. I allowed him to work his way free from my hold while still keeping the invisible safety net of my arms and legs directly underneath his tiny body.

Once I let go, an amazing thing happened. Trey did a sort of dog-paddle-combination breast stroke which projected him straight to the edge of the pool; his first attempt and he was swimming. It was truly amazing. He did this over and over, and even pushed off the side of the pool in order to move further each time, the whole while with me, just under his reach. He never touched me and never became winded. He just paddled his way back and forth across the pool.

Stunned, I looked to the swim coach. "I can't believe it; how does he know how to swim?"

The coach looked at me with a smile and said, "He has been watching his sister for weeks, of course he knows how to swim."

That one defining moment changed the way I taught my children, as well as the way I managed my team at work. I realized there was no need to spell everything out for my children, they had been watching and learning by my husband's and my example. Hopefully, by our own illustration and our model, they would know how to behave, to move forward, and to respond to difficulty.

Hopefully, they would need very little direction, since they had been, watching all along.

Chapter 46

For Others

"If we did all the things we are capable of, we would literally astound ourselves." Thomas A. Edison

A young man, in our small town, who was on the city football team became seriously injured in a car accident. Justin had a long and difficult recovery, but his team rallied around him. Realizing his full recovery would take months, and he would not return that season, the team decided to dedicate the remainder of the season to their injured teammate. With every game they spoke of Justin in the locker room and how their goal was to enter the play-offs in his honor. They put his initials on their helmets as a reminder of their goal. On the rare occasion, when Justin would attend a game, and watch from the stands, they would point to him after a winning play and chant his name.

The team rallied that season, playing for Justin helped them play with cohesion and solidarity. They won every game and made the playoffs. They fought long and hard in the playoff games and took the series. The state championship followed, and Justin's team was now on a greater mission. During the state championship game, the team continuously chanted their teammates name at every opportunity.

They won that night, and when the award ceremony occurred, the trophy was presented to the coach. The coach walked up into the stands into the cheering crowd. He found Justin, at the top of the stands, wrapped in a blanket in the last seat. "This is for you!" The coach smiled, handing the State Championship trophy to this injured young man.

"I can't accept this, coach," the player said softly.

"You taught this team how to work toward a goal for someone other than themselves, and that is a life lesson they will always remember. This trophy belongs to you, see you out there next year!" the coach exclaimed.

That same, small town team went on to win the State Championship for three straight years, because they learned the power of true teamwork.

Chapter 47

Trey's Character

"It is easier to build strong children than to repair broken men." Frederick Douglass

My son participated in wrestling from elementary school age through middle school. He became an amazing wrestler and right before one of his middle school matches, he jogged over to his father and me in the stands. "One of my coaches asked me not to point to the sky before I wrestle," he told us. "He says it doesn't really help me, and I don't need to do it."

My husband started to rise out of his chair to address this with his coach. I put my hand on his arm to imply I would take a stab at the response. "Trey, this is one of those moments in life that defines you. You can honor your coach and we will respect your decision, or you can choose to honor your faith and we will respect that decision as well," I told him. Trey nodded and ran back to his team. At that moment, the outcome of the match did not matter to me. Instead, I knew my son had to make a difficult choice. My money was on Trey's faith, but the jury was still out.

A few minutes later, my son's name was called, and he ran onto the mat. This time, instead of his normal very subtle point to the heavens, indicating this one is for you God, my son changed it up. This time, he pointed to the heavens with a bold, strong hand, one to suggest no more subtleness about it; a point his coach couldn't miss.

I don't even remember if Trey won or lost his match that day, what I do remember was he won his character.

Chapter 48

Apple Pie from the Farm

"Creativity is intelligence having fun." Albert Einstein

Mom often visited the elderly and brought them homemade meals. She always made sure they had a delicious, hot meal with every food group represented and always included a dessert. What I noticed most were her finishing touches. The drinks would be wrapped in foil, to keep them cold, the trays would always have a flowered paper napkin, the beautiful ones she would use for fancy parties. She always finished the preparation of each tray with a bright cheerful flower. "They are our elders and should be treasured," she often reminded me. I watched as she delivered the meals and treated our elderly in the community like royalty.

The first thing the recipients always said as mom greeted them with the tray was, "Look at the beautiful napkin, is this really for me?"

"Made especially for you," Mom smiled.

Mom frequently visited a dear friend, who was in a nursing home, who suffered from Alzheimer's Disease. On one of my Mom's visits, she noticed Gracie wasn't eating, and the staff was growing frustrated as she became thinner. My mom, knowing Gracie since she was young, asked the staff if she could try to feed her the prepared lunch. Mom sat next to Gracie and I watched as the magic unfolded.

"How's the farm, Gracie?" Mom asked, while scooping the macaroni. Mom held the spoon up to Gracie's lips and kept talking about Gracie's childhood as if they slipped back in time together. Gracie listened attentively, and slowly opened her mouth, completely distracted by my mom's words. Mom continued to provide small spoonsful's of food and Gracie continued to listen and eat. She even answered a few of Mom's questions about the animals and people on the farm where Gracie had been raised.

When Gracie had finished the meal, Mom said, "Have some dessert, it is apple pie, your mom made this for you. I believe you picked the apples yourself."

Gracie ate the pie with gusto, nodding her head and smiling from ear to ear, as she remembered picking apples as a child. I watched in awe as Mom and Gracie shared a meal and a moment in time. The entire staff watched in amazement as Gracie ate her first full meal in weeks. I have always admired Mom's quick thinking that day. She was a hero, not just to Gracie, but to me.

Chapter 49

A Shared Voice

"In order to carry a positive action, we must develop here a positive vision." Dalai Lama

We pulled into the church parking lot and Trey asked, "What does this entail again?"

"Don't worry." I smiled. "Look at all the volunteers, you might not even be selected, I just want you to offer your services." Trey's ninth-grade self begrudgingly agreed, as he slowly walked inside the reception area of the church. It was there he met Mike, an autistic eighth grader who couldn't speak. Twelve teenagers stood in a circle around Michael and his mother, who was speaking for him as he pointed to letters on a board, spelling out his sentences. They greeted us and asked the young volunteers to talk about their interests and hobbies, so Mike could listen to their voices.

Mike and his family were seeking someone near Mike's age to be a voice donor. When Mike typed his words into a unique computer, the computer would speak the words he was spelling, and allow people to hear Mike's words. The goal was to have a voice Mike liked, rather than a machine's voice speak as he typed his sentences.

The choice for Mike's voice would be made by Mike in a tournament like selection. Mike's Mom, Lori, explained the process to the volunteers. "Mike will listen to each of you say a few sentences, something about yourselves. Talk a little about your hobbies or interests, and Mike will narrow it down until he makes his final choice." Mike also noted as he typed, he was so grateful for all those who were volunteering, and he did not want to hurt anyone's feelings in this process if they were not selected, he just had an idea of the voice he was hoping to represent his typing.

Trey thought about what to say quietly. He spoke about his love of coding, and how he played lacrosse. Trey and seven others made it through the first round. The audition continued and Trey spoke about his cats. Each time Trey spoke, he modified his sentence or added a clarification, sometimes he stumbled to find the words. He was so earnest and endearing, honestly, I was so proud of Trey for trying, for offering his voice, even if he was not selected. I was unsure if Trey would make it to the next round.

The second round, the third, and finally, Trey was still standing with two other young volunteers. Mike's mom addressed the remaining three young men. "I just want you to understand what is required for this process. This is no easy task. It will require about sixty hours of meticulous voice recording. You will need to read several thousand sentences and repeat them into a microphone until each one is recorded, exactly correct. Are you remaining young men okay with this?" she asked.

Trey looked over his shoulder at me and shot me a panicked look. He was not much of a reader, but more of an audio-visual processor. Reading was not his first choice for an activity. "If this doesn't sound like something you would like to do, now is the time to say so," Mike's mom continued.

Trey stood stock still and stayed in the running. "Tell us about the sports you play." Mike typed as his Mother read his keyboard. The three young men continued, and Mike typed quickly on to his keyboard. "t-h-the b-o-boy i-n-in t-h-the y-e-l-l" and before his mom could finish the sentence Trey looked down at his shirt. It was yellow. He had been chosen. The boy in the yellow shirt!

Both shocked and horrified at the selection, Trey graciously accepted. Mike typed out his *thank you's* to the other young men, and while a few of them crowded around him, Mike's mom walked over to me. "I want to share something with you," she whispered. "When we started this process, I asked Mike how he planned to select a voice, he told me he planned to pick the boy with a pure heart, and he wanted the voice that sounded the most like the voice he heard when he spoke in his dreams."

I choked back tears and hugged her. "He certainty did select the young man with a pure heart, that is my Trey," I whispered back.

We walked back to the car, me beaming with pride and Trey shaking his head and mumbling, "Sixty hours."

A few weeks later, Trey was settled in the middle of our basement, surrounded by sheets on the windows to block out any vibrations of sound, and furniture moved to the walls to reduce any echo. Trey used a special microphone Mike's family bought for him, to connect with his computer. The first sentence Trey spoke into the microphone was, "Toto, we're not in Kansas anymore." The computer rang out, "Not accepted, please read again." And he did just that. He read each and every sentence over and over as many times as necessary. This task was to be completed with absolutely no noise, no vibrations from the computer, or noise from any place in the house.

"Guys! Can you be a little quieter?" Trey would yell upstairs to us, if we disrupted his process. As Trey spoke into the microphone, he started understanding the process. I asked him how he felt about his commitment.

"At first, I was worried I wouldn't do a good job and I began to realize how important this job really was. I talk every day, probably too much, and I could never imagine a life without a voice. To know something, but not be able to share it, to not be able to speak your mind, or voice your opinion, to not be able to tell a joke, or stand up for yourself. I was on a greater mission than I realized, and the more I thought about it, the more I wanted to do the best job I possibly could," Trey said confidently.

After that initial process, Trey's commitment was strengthened. There were times when Trey was asked to enhance or to add more verbiage. Trey accepted wholeheartedly. Trey even recorded the Lord's Prayer, so Mike could "recite it," for his aunt's wedding.

This opportunity enhanced Trey's career path. Trey knew he loved computer science, and wanted to major in computer science in college, but now there was a reason behind the decision. This experience helped Trey realize, technology can be used for the greater good.

Mike and Trey may not be brothers. They don't share parents, but they share a voice, and they will always be family.

Chapter 50

Live Among the Young

"It takes a long time to become young." Pablo Picasso

Mom always said it takes a village. It is amazing to me how she still manages to live in a typical suburban community. When we suggest she may want to move to a nursing home, she squints and says, "Why, I live here perfectly, and my house paid in full. Helen brings young Callie and toddler Mabel over to visit; what a joy. The young children in the neighborhood Leyna, Roxie, and Violette, stop over on their way home from school. The young boys next door, Liam and Jack, bring me my mail, Laura takes my trash to the curb, Julie and Scott share their delicious meals with me, at least once a week, and Dick and Scott drive me to the hairdresser. Calvin fixes my roof, Michelle brings me candy and Eric even invited me to his Prom. I surround myself with friends. Not those who cannot, but those who can; they lift my spirits."

"But what if something happens?" I asked her.

"Jennifer, if my blinds do not open in the morning, the neighbors who live behind me, the Sullivans or Ms. Lynch will call me immediately. If my paper doesn't get picked up, Jessica stops to check on me. Why would I move where everyone is old? I am young in spirit and it keeps me young to be involved in everyone's life here. I am so blessed."

I spoke with Mom one gloomy Saturday morning, Mom noted how she was a little blue that day. With back-to-back events for my family that day, I called my sister, Janell, and asked if she could stop by and check on Mom. She ran over, only to find there was nowhere to park. Mom had company, and the driveway was full of cars.

Janell walked into Mom's house to find Mom entertaining two couples, who had stopped by on their way out of town. Tea and chocolate chip cookies were being served and Janell stood while everyone conversed. After they left, Janell asked Mom if she had been blue.

"Only for a short while, but then the sun came out, I went out on the porch, ran into some friends and forgot I was lonely," Mom replied.

When you are feeling blue, get out of the house, get out of your room, go outside and bask in nature, take a walk, go talk to someone or, better yet, do something for someone else. There is no greater cure for loneliness. Socialization can help your memory, work your muscles, and lift your spirit. Even in her late 90s, Mom's voice has always been that of a young person. I believe it is because she uses it so frequently. There are times when she may repeat a story, but I make sure I always listen again, and act surprised at the outcome. I never want her to think I was ever asking her not to talk. Her voice shows her youthful and loving spirit.

Chapter 51

Knights of Rhythm

"Music can change the world, because it can change people." Bono

One afternoon, while driving my mom home from the hairdresser's, I asked her if she could have any job, and money wasn't a consideration or worry, what job would she desire. I thought she might respond with, a real estate salesperson, something she did for forty years, or maybe the president of a corporation. She pondered only for a moment and looked at me with a sparkle in her eye and whispered, "The lead singer in a band."

I had no idea. I inquired further and she noted she had been in a band in high school, called the *Knights of Rhythm*. She described how it made her feel to sing her heart out and have people sing along and cheer. I realized my mom had so much more to her than just being my mom, she was a performer. Now I knew why her family was so outgoing and loved to perform. Mom's response also reminded me not to take yourself too seriously and to dare to dream.

I have no doubt, one day, if I am blessed enough to enter Heaven, I will hear the exquisite voice of a beautiful blonde in stiletto heels, belting out a glorious song, as she leads her magnificent band.

Chapter 52

One Conversation with Katelyn

"A single conversation across the table with a wise man is better than ten years mere study of books." Henry Wadsworth Longfellow

After my dad died, my siblings and I wanted to do something to honor his memory at Christmas time. We decided to volunteer at a home for battered and abused children. When we arrived to celebrate bringing toys and gifts, we mentioned we were there in memory of our father, James Girardi.

"That's a familiar name," said the woman at the front desk. "I think your dad was one of our volunteers. He came to help with his church group." Dad had indeed worked around the home painting and fixing things with some of the men from his Knights of Columbus group at our church. This was very comforting to know and made us feel as if he was there with us. We decided we would make this our holiday tradition. We had my brother, Jim, dress as Santa and distribute gifts, we would play with the children and celebrate with them and we would facilitate a

Christmas carol sing-along, initiated by my sister-in-law, Marylee.

We decided each adult who volunteered with us, would focus on one child at the home and give them personal one-on-one attention. It was fun to open their presents with them and listen as they shared their excitement. Some children, wanted a book read to them, others just wanted someone to help them put their new socks on their feet.

Mariah had been volunteering at this home with us, since she was a baby. One particular year, Mariah took her role to heart and was about seven years old and in elementary school, when she met Katelyn. Mariah opened presents with Katelyn and the two talked for hours as the party erupted around them. Katelyn was Mariah's age and the two seemed lost in conversation.

I looked over at one point to see Mariah deeply engrossed in what appeared to be a quiet heart-to-heart conversation with Katelyn. I never asked her what the conversation was about, but I would eventually find out the impact that day had on my daughter. We went back to the facility year after year and Katelyn was no longer living there. Mariah would ask if there was any information about Katelyn, how she was doing, where she was. No information was provided.

Years later, Mariah was writing her college application essay. She chose to write about Katelyn. What she had not told us was that Katelyn told Mariah that December morning, that she did not want to go home. This shelter offered a safe place for children to reside to protect them until their parents obtained the required skill set needed for their children to return home. Mariah was not sure of the specifics, but she knew Katelyn did not feel safe in her home, she knew there was so much more to the story.

Without mentioning this to anyone, Mariah created *The Katelyn Project*. As a freshman in high school, she had started a blog, raised money for a local church to give to victims of human trafficking, and encouraged young people to respond online, talk about their situations, ask for support, and donate their time and money to help victims who had been abused. The blog was full of articles she had found on abuse, what signs to look for in your friends, and where to reach out for help.

I had no idea she had done all this and didn't realize its impact until I read her college application essay where she described her project in detail. I looked at the blog and all the responses it had received, and I discovered she had initiated the project because of her discussion with Katelyn, early one December morning.

Today, my amazing daughter, Mariah, is in her third year of college where she is studying International Relations with a double major in Economics. Her goal is to help others in every way she can, including helping the fight against human trafficking.

Mariah's humble approach was the most selfless act. Her humility has inspired my direction.

Chapter 53

Her Name Starts with an "S"

"For it is in giving that we receive." Francis of Assisi

Living on the East Coast, my husband loved to take our family hiking on the Appalachian Trail. One spring evening, on a hiking trip with our son, Keith and Trey stopped at a campground and shared stories and dinner with the other hikers. At this campsite, they met a young woman who seemed less than prepared. Keith noticed her shoes were like sandals rather than the closed-toed hiking boots most hikers wore. Her gear did not include a sleeping bag, but instead, she had a blanket and a tarp. He also noticed she had a very limited food supply. Trey and Keith both wondered if perhaps she was running from something.

The next morning, after they met her, I received a phone call from Keith. "Hey Babe," he began, "Trey and I are great, and we are looking so forward to you and Mariah picking us up today, but when you come, can you do me a favor?" Keith continued, "Can you bring the extra sleeping bag, the camp stove, the extra backpack in the garage, and Trey's new sneakers?" Keith went on to explain about this woman and how she did not have the gear she needed for her trek. He explained how it made Trey and him feel and how they wanted to help. Mariah and I gathered all the gear Keith had requested and we added granola bars, candy, and even added a book for this young woman.

When we reached the pickup location that afternoon, Mariah and I watched as Keith came from the trail limping, with his arm around Trey. Keith has twisted his knee and was struggling to reach the rendezvous point. Trey was full of strength and energy, ready to carry his dad, if needed. Keith insisted he was fine, but was worried he would not be able to continue hiking to deliver the young woman's gear.

Mariah and I split up all the gear we had gathered for her and asked the guys where this woman was heading, assuring them that we would make the delivery. Keith knew her proposed next location, so we headed there via car. This location was unique because, a sort of welcome center existed, so fortunately we could drive right up to the door.

The gentleman who manned the center approached us as we headed toward the entrance. We explained our goal, and I turned and asked Keith the name of the woman we were searching for. "Her name begins with an S," he whispered. Here we had ventured to bring gear to a new friend, and we were not even sure of the name of the person for whom we were searching. Keith and the welcome center man played through a series of female names starting with an "S."

"Sarah?"

"No!"

"Sally?"

"Nope."

"Stephanie?"

"Stephanie! That's it," Keith shouted!

The welcome center gentleman told us Stephanie had planned to hike a little further and we could find her a few miles away, at a specific location. We propped Keith's knee up and Trey tended to his dad's injury in the car. Mariah and I set off, with Keith and Trey's directions in our pocket and arms full of gear. We headed deep into the trail. Not only were we not positive of this young woman's name, we were not sure what she looked like or where she would be. None of that mattered, we continued on.

We hiked past a water tower on our right, only to determine the tower should have been on our left, but after many switchbacks and a few missed turns, we found the path to Stephanie. We approached a young woman, sitting by herself wearing sandals, and next to her was a tarp she had slung over a low branch. "Stephanie?" I asked as we drew nearer to her.

She was reluctant to answer since she had no idea who we were or why we were addressing her. She quietly lifted her head and rose cautiously to her feet. I quickly explained we were the sent by Keith and Trey to provide her with some gear she may have been missing. Her trepidation shifted to delight as she tried on the shoes, which fit her perfectly and she seemed genuinely pleased about the sleeping bag, camp stove, backpack, and food.

As Mariah and I hiked back to the car, neither of us spoke, we just relished in the knowledge that we had the ability to give a little comfort to someone we would never see again. We were grateful to be the deliverers of Keith's wonderful idea, and even more grateful we could share her delight with the guys on our return. Keith's example of giving to someone, even though you would never see them again, was a beautiful illustration to all of us, never hesitate, just give.

Chapter 54

Strength in Standing

"If I have seen further than others, it is by standing upon the shoulders of giants." Isaac Newton

One rainy afternoon, I raced to my son's junior varsity high school lacrosse game. I arrived early, in time to catch the last quarter of the varsity game. The game was ongoing, so in an effort not to block anyone's view, I sat in the first seat I could find in the bleachers, which happened to be in the opposing team's section. My thought was to wait for a time out or break and move to the home team's side of the stands. The varsity home team was ahead by five goals. "Another goal for number three from the home team!" the announcer rang out. He then followed with the statistics of each home team player who had scored and a quick nickname or fun fact about the home team member he was addressing. Accolades flew for each effort made by the home team.

When the opposing team made a goal the announcer simple noted, "Goal by the opposing team." No name was associated with the goal or any mention of the assist or effort by the opposing team's players.

After three-quarters of a rainy game, with little recognition for the visiting team, a few members of the visiting team's student body started to whisper among themselves. The whispers grew throughout the stands and soon almost forty teens had risen to their feet. With complete control and respect, they started to cheer for their team. Every time a goal was made by their team, they would shout out the goal maker's name and offer praise and recognition to the teammates. They simply stood for the remainder of the game, and were very courteous when the home team scored, but they were very excited when their visiting team scored.

The visiting team spectators did not sit down. It was as if the players could feel the difference. The visiting team played hard and strong, and they went from a once five-point discrepancy, to a tied score. The game went into overtime and double over time. The opposing team's students in the stands remained vigilant and on their feet. Finally, the referees announced sudden-death, and the visiting team students became even louder than ever. They seemed to spark the giants on the field, and on that rainy afternoon, the visiting team scored and won a very difficult and trying game.

The home team was amazed. They were expected to win this game, and up until the fourth quarter, they were winning. However, one student sparked another, and a flame was ignited to send the underdogs into an inexplicable victory.

Those teens taught me something that day, and although my team lost that game, I learned the most valuable lesson of hope, spirit, and belief.

Don't wait for the miracle, be the miracle.

Chapter 55

What is the Recipe?

"In the sweetness of friendship let there be laughter and sharing of pleasures. For in the dew of little things the heart finds its morning and is refreshed." Khalil Gibran

My in-laws, Jim and Linda McCloskey, were visiting and we were discussing their upcoming fiftieth wedding anniversary. *Wow,* I remember thinking, *what an accomplishment to celebrate a fifty-year anniversary.* Knowing them for over twenty years, I've watched as they celebrated their lives and lived through joy and pain, as they watched their children marry and as they buried their parents, and everything in between. They were a beautiful example to everyone, of commitment and love. Diving a little deeper I asked them one morning, "What is the recipe for a fifty-year marriage?"

Thinking there may be a secret formula or a special mantra they carried with them, I awaited their response. They glanced at each other and ginned, in an instant, my mother-in-law spoke up and said with a big smile,

"Laughter!" My father-in-law agreed, nodding with a hearty laugh, as he reached for a hug from his wife.

Laughing at yourself, at a situation, and with each other has proven to be the best medicine for any relationship. I was thrilled the recipe was simple and easy, I will strive to implement their advice in my life every day. I promise to laugh much and often.

Chapter 56

What Would I do...

"I learned that courage was not the absence of fear, but the triumph over it. The brave man is not he who does not feel afraid, but he who conquers that fear." Nelson Mandela

My daughter came home from a leadership forum one day, and told us the theme they had considered that weekend. Being a student of leadership and its forms and benefits, I expected her to mention something about being a wise leader or offer a mantra perhaps, something similar to, *paper is managed, but people are led.* But instead, she brought home a simple sentence which forever changed my life. Her theme for the weekend was, in fact, a question, "What would I do if I were brave?"

She noted how they were all challenged to think of ways they would make a difference, and be brave in their decisions and in their support of doing what was right. Their weekend was based on a song by Jana Stanfield and Jimmy Scott, and I vowed to make her mantra one I would continue. She even taught me how to use American Sign

163

Language and sign the phrase in case we were in a room where we couldn't hear each other. She knew she could sign the phrase, "What would I do if I were brave?" and I would know it was time for action. Thank you, Mariah for teaching your mother to be brave, I am forever grateful.

Chapter 57

Pull Over, Pull Over!

"A hero is no braver than an ordinary man, but he is brave five minutes longer." Ralph Waldo Emerson

"Pull over, pull over!" my husband, Keith, shouted as we passed a car facing the opposite direction on the highway.

We had barely avoided a collision with the car ourselves and were shocked to see a woman still inside. As cars careened around the corner of a highway on-ramp tucked under a bridge, her car was unable to move. It had hit the barrier and was turned around, now facing oncoming traffic in the fast lane of the highway.

I pulled my car to the left shoulder and Keith leapt into action. With only moments to spare, he ran toward her, "Are you okay?" he asked quickly, while heading toward the top of the ramp.

Seeing she was fine, but shaken, he immediately raced to the merge area to signal oncoming cars to avoid her lane. He was in the moment, and his every action was to work quickly, so no one else was hurt. He used the light on his cell phone to signal other drivers to move to the opposite lane. Everyone exiting the ramp was driving at least fifty-five MPH, and he needed to act fast, so another accident did not occur.

Realizing the woman was fine, just shaken, I helped her from her car, and out of the way of oncoming traffic. We called 911 and waited for the police to arrive. The area where we waited, was under the bridge with little room for error. We watched as every car merging onto the ramp barely missed her. I suggested we move to a safer location, but she was too shaken and wanted to stay near her car. As we watched cars whizzing by, we silently hoped no one would hit her car, which was still in the fast lane and not visible as the lanes merged onto the ramp. Keith continued to warn drivers with his arms waving and cell phone light in motion. Our safety ultimately depended on his continued dedication to the task.

Police and rescue workers soon arrived, and the woman was found to have no injuries. The police asked how long we had waited for them to arrive. Once we noted the time, they were in disbelief. How was it possible no one was injured, and another car had not hit her car, tucked backwards, right in the middle of the fast lane?

My husband jumped into action that day, without a thought for his own safety and without fear. It was as if he was still a Boy Scout waiting for his opportunity to assist.

He was not only prepared, he was ready and willing.

Chapter 58

Refrigerator University

"Only I can change my life. No one can do it for me." Carol Burnett

As a mother of two children and a motivational speaker, I am sure my children often think, *Oh please, Mom, enough talk about how things work together for good, enough reminders of how being rained on is good luck or how we can learn something from everyone.* So, in an effort to eliminate preaching to my children, I have resorted to something I call *Refrigerator University.*

I place a piece of paper with a quote I love or a quick lesson on the refrigerator, with a magnet, and I change it out weekly. I know my children, Mariah and Trey will frequent the refrigerator anywhere between 1 and 368 times each day, opening it to see if perhaps I have added something new to the selection. My goal is for them to read the quote, and hopefully make it their own.

That goal was met one morning when I placed a quote my husband, Keith, had found front and center on the fridge. My husband, being concerned with fitness and health,

167

found the following quote that read, "You can be sore tomorrow, or you can be sorry tomorrow. The choice is yours."

After the quote had been displayed on the refrigerator for a few days, my daughter received a phone call from a friend. I heard Mariah repeating the words, "Look you don't need to come to cheerleading practice tonight, but I know you will regret it if you don't come. You can be sore tomorrow, or you can be sorry tomorrow. The choice is yours."

Her brilliant mind processed the quote and passed it onto a friend. I thought to myself, *she deserves a diploma from Refrigerator University.*

Chapter 59

Thank You

"The hardest arithmetic to master is that which enables us to count our blessings." Eric Hoffer

"The world belongs to people who write 'Thank You' notes," Mom would say. If someone took the time to bring you something, they deserve a "Thank You" note. Verbal approval is wonderful; however, a handwritten note is magnificent. Everyone reads the handwritten notes from their mailbox first.

Mom also reminded me, if someone sends you a meal or a dessert and you need to return the plate, never return the plate empty. Send a few cookies along with the return, you are sure to brighten their day, and return a genuine *thank you*.

Chapter 60

The Sweater

I had my dad's Army sweater dry-cleaned, in the hope it would be fresh and useful to someone. The sweater, once found in the basement, which triggered so many memories for my family, was now draped in a drycleaner's clear bag, hung gently on the door of Mom's kitchen. The sweater hung there for a few months. No one in the family wanted to part with the memory-laden sweater, but none of us dared to wear it. It seemed almost sacred.

My daughter, Mariah, was nineteen at the time, and had come home from college on Thanksgiving break. She ran through Mom's front door and into her kitchen, hugging her grandmother firmly, while kissing her cheek. "Hi-Grams!" she shouted, "I have missed you so much!" My mom was thrilled to see Mariah, and immediately showered her with praise and accolades. As Mariah answered every question Grams threw her way, her eyes silently scanned the kitchen and fell upon the now nearly eighty-year-old wool sweater.

"What's this?" Mariah asked, gently removing the garment from the bag. "This is awesome," she said, turning it over in her hands and pressing the fabric to her cheek for a moment. "What cool material."

Mom smiled, looking over at me and said, "It's your grandfather's Army sweater. Pop-Pop would be so honored if you wore it. Would you like to have it?"

"Are you kidding? Of course!" Mariah replied, excitedly.

In an instant, the sweater which was once so pristine, was pulled over my daughter's head. It complimented her cute jeans and stylish shoes making the ensemble look incredibly vintage and fashionable on this nineteen-year-old.

"Mom, are you sure?" I whispered, noting the importance of the sweater.

Mom grinned at me and simply said, "Now the sweater has a whole new generation of stories to begin, and memories to make."

Conclusion

This book is meant as a reminder of the numerous heroes around us. I have always been surprised by the number of books sold depicting pain and heartache. I wanted my children to read real stories about people who succeeded through trying times, and how they had mastered the art of obtaining resources, embracing teamwork, and garnering inner strength, while working toward a greater good; something greater than themselves. My goal, is to remind us we all have living legends, currently surrounding us. We don't need to look only to the famous or the wealthy as our models of strength, but we can observe inner strength through our daily interactions, even in our own households, maybe in the next room.

A lesson can be learned from the father or mother who continues to make their long commute into the office, day after day, so they can provide financial support for their family, while providing emotional support to a son or daughter, who may be struggling in school or with their friends. Some of those parents work multiple jobs, and still find the strength to lend an ear or wipe away tears. An example can be seen in the parent or coworker who is slow to anger, always seeking to find ways to prevent arguments, while still maintaining order and a path forward for their family or team.

We are surrounded by living legends. If we can't see them, all we need to do is open our eyes a little wider.

About the Author

Jennifer McCloskey has been a Motivational Speaker and trainer across the country since 1986. Her workshops have been well received by several corporations, churches, athletic communities, and numerous high schools throughout the United States.

Three of Jennifer's seminars were also used in India. She has been a keynote speaker at numerous events. Jennifer was the feature of a CBS Evening News story on Women in Non-traditional Roles.

She has also been the subject of several newspaper articles highlighting her career.

Jennifer is a volunteer at a home for battered and abused children, near Washington DC.

She also authored a, "Dear Abby," type advice column for community teens.

Although she is trained as a Civil Engineer, her favorite role is as a wife and mother of two children, who loves being with her family and sparking the light within others.

Acknowledgements

Thank you to my Dad who taught me the true meaning of fortitude, and to my Mom who loved me always and unconditionally. Thank you for the beautiful examples you have provided for me and my family to follow.

I would like to express my very sincere thanks to my husband, Keith who believed in me since the day we met.

I would also like to thank my daughter, Mariah and my son, Trey for living their lives in a way that continues to inspire me.

Thank you to the best siblings in the world, Jim, Mike, and Janell, my sister-in-laws Marylee, Nina, and Gabrielle, and my brother-in-law Kurt.

Thank you for being so much fun as I watched you grow, Jim, Jenny, Erin, Chris, Amy, Josh, and Sam.

I look so forward to watching you grow, Bryan, Abigail, Maddie, Ella, Quinn, Skye, Julian, Auguste, Aven, and Wes.

Thank you to my cousin John Rey and my niece Erin who inspired me to write these stories down.

Thank you to my Mom's neighbors who have kept her young at heart, I will never be able to repay all the love you have given her. You have kept her strong all these years, and I am forever grateful. Thank you,

Helen, Mike, Callie, and Mabel Maurer

Laura, Jonathan, Jack and Liam Bodner

Julie, Scott, Leyna, Roxie, and Violette Weismantel

Margaret, Calvin, Sarah, Eric, Anna, Paige and Mitch Meleney

Debbie, Dick, Melissa, Rob, and Chris Van Alstyne

Barbara, Jim, Julie, Steve, and Betsy Lynch

Chelle Davis

Michele, Faith, and Ellie Meyer

Ruth Abakah

Valerie Cole

Juno Barber

Selam Kifletsion

Cecilia Mostafá, Arturo, Amira, and Tareq Giadala

Dee Bogart

Pat and Joe Doane

Bill Duvall

A special thanks to Susan Bierly who reminds me every day the meaning of true friendship.

Thank you to Nancy Vawter for always being there for me, not just in words, but in actions.

Thank you to Beverly Tucker for her listening heart and her continued support.

Thank you to Marcy Rindone whose courage during her illness was inspirational to all of us.

A special thanks to Reesi Buell-Size who showed me how to have a backbone when learning about relationships, I am so very grateful. You gave me some of the best memories of my life.

Thank you to Jenny Roussos whose beautiful heart taught me how to laugh out loud!

To Jenny Duncan my friend and clothing twin, thanks for teaching me to spell.

Thank you to Kathleen Crowley who taught me to roller-skate while walking her dog and how to perform on stage.

Special thanks to Betsy Lanning for being an amazing example of love and kindness toward her mother.

A giant thank you goes out to Donna McCullough and Vonna Ordaz, may they know they have always been there when I needed them most.

Thank you to Cris Packard and Nancy Lao who have celebrated every meaningful event in my children's life with me.

Thank you to Loretta Brooks for sharing your love of speaking, and inviting me to the seminar where I met my editor.

To Lil Barcaski, the most amazing editor, writer, and friend, whose work on this book made it come to life. Thank you, Lil, for making my dream a reality.

A special thanks to Erin Girardi for her brilliance on my cover, thank you Erin for listening to my heart and making it come to life.

CPSIA information can be obtained
at www.ICGtesting.com
Printed in the USA
BVHW041949101219
566229BV00015B/281/P